MW00643985

PERSUASIVE

PERSUASIVE

40 Lessons in Communicating
for the Common Good

MARRIANNE MCMULLEN

Georgetown University Press / Washington, DC

The publisher is not responsible for third-party websites or their content. URL links were active at time of publication.

Library of Congress Cataloging-in-Publication Data

Names: McMullen, Marrianne, 1960- author.
Title: Persuasive : 40 lessons from a career in communicating for the common good / Marrianne McMullen.
Description: Washington, DC : Georgetown University Press, 2024. | Includes bibliographical references and index.
Identifiers: LCCN 2023040848 (print) | LCCN 2023040849 (ebook) | ISBN 9781647124656 (hardcover) | ISBN 9781647124649 (ebook)
Subjects: LCSH: McMullen, Marrianne, 1960- | Journalists—United States—Biography. | Public relations personnel—United States—Biography. | Business communication—United States. | Communication in politics—United States. | Persuasion (Psychology) | LCGFT: Autobiographies.
Classification: LCC PN4874.M463 A3 2024 (print) | LCC PN4874.M463 (ebook) | DDC 070.92 [B]—dc23/eng/20230920
LC record available at https://lccn.loc.gov/2023040848
LC ebook record available at https://lccn.loc.gov/2023040849

∞ This paper meets the requirements of ANSI/NISO Z39.48-1992 (Permanence of Paper).

25 24   9 8 7 6 5 4 3 2 First printing

Printed in the United States of America

Cover design by Faceout Studio, Amanda Hudson
Interior design by Paul Hotvedt

To Jeff, who makes all the best things in my life possible.

Contents

Illustrations

Preface

It was still winter in April on the Spirit Lake Reservation in North Dakota. The shell of a car was perched on the ice of the frozen lake. When warmer temperatures thinned the ice and the car sank, that would be the public signal that spring had begun. Two of my Obama administration colleagues and I were in a car with Tribal Chairman Russ MacDonald that spring of 2014 when he explained the purpose behind the abandoned vehicle. We were on a fact-finding trip to look into rising reports of child maltreatment on the reservation. For the moment, though, I was distracted by the foul image of a heap of cars rusting at the bottom of the lake.

Three months later I would be at Lackland Air Force Base in the arid heat of Texas, managing media and community relations related to 1,000 unaccompanied migrant children living on the base. An office in my division of the US Department of Health and Human Services was responsible for caring for the teenagers until their US-based family and friends could take custody of them.

Through these and dozens of other experiences shared in the following pages, I've learned the nuances of effective work in communications. I learned about journalism as I interviewed dissidents from behind the Iron Curtain in the early '80s. I learned about crisis communications from Neil Young and about public speaking when I had to do an impromptu toast to Bianca Jagger at an international climate conference. And I learned from engaging in public battles with Catholic bishops over reproductive rights and from crafting strategy for insuring millions of people under the Affordable Care Act.

These stories from my journalism and public affairs career, and the lessons taught by each, are shared in the following 40 short chapters. While primarily a professional memoir, this is also a personal story with two distinct themes. One is of class mobility: I am a second-generation American from a working-class family. My people were rooted in their place in Pittsburgh, but it was a place I decided to leave, ending up in professional circles with few others from my background. That class diaspora became more pronounced as my career led me into workplaces populated by Ivy League elites, requiring me to develop tactics to build my credibility and affirm my own sense of who I was as a person and a professional.

Another personal theme is rooted in my foster-parenting experience with a family of six girls. I was only in my 20s when I met and fell in love with them. Their parents had abandoned them, and their grandparents were raising them. I provided counseling, shelter, recreation, respite care, and foster care for them over a decade, but they stayed in my life for good. My experiences with them, and the devastating consequences of their trauma, impacted my life and my career in unexpected ways.

My work as a professional communicator began in journalism. I later moved into nonprofit communications, particularly with labor unions, then into government communications with DC Public Schools and the Obama administration. And then, finally, I went on to academia as the communication director of a research center, Chapin Hall at the University of Chicago. Communications is the throughline. The ability to write one clear, intelligible sentence after another proved to be career bread and butter. Understanding communication strategy and developing management skills moved me along a path to positions of greater responsibility. All the while, my family of foster children, godchildren, and my one biological son, intersected with, and even drove, my professional life.

My experiences led me to write a book that is, first and foremost, meant to be useful. Hundreds of thousands of us, in the United States alone, work full time in communications. But communication touches every profession. The ability to do it well, in any field, is often what separates line workers from management.

The start of a career often includes critical lessons about the work you have chosen and about yourself. This is the focus of "Foundations," the first part of the book. During my first decade in journalism, I reported on the punishing dangers of coal liquefaction. I stayed in a garage with no plumbing or electricity while reporting on conditions that led to an FBI siege at Mohawk Nation. And I experienced a "stop the presses" moment at an afternoon daily when the space shuttle *Challenger* exploded. In these first seven chapters, I share the lessons I learned that would influence the rest of my career.

The second part describes running the alternative newsweekly the *Dayton Voice*. My husband, Jeff Epton, and I ran a scrappy paper in an even scrappier city on a shoestring, all while we raised a family of foster daughters, I finished my graduate degree in communications, and then eventually we had our own child, Brendan. But the *stories* we did. One led to the release of two wrongfully convicted people serving life sentences in prison. Others led to the firing of corrupt officials and held public institutions accountable. And the workplace culture we built informed my management style for decades.

Equipped with a graduate degree and nearly two decades in communications, I started working in the labor movement, which is part three of the book. Labor communications challenges ranged from fighting major hospital chains to getting Barack Obama elected to the US Senate. Adventures ranged from organizing a daylong outdoor rock concert in Minneapolis to serving as a labor delegate to the United Nations climate talks. Exposure to communication theory led to my development of the Persuasion Matrix, a model that I would go on to use throughout my career to plan effective communication campaigns. These nine chapters reflect that increasingly sophisticated approach.

Part four of the book is focused on school reform. I wrestled with Dayton Public Schools over my foster kids, reported on the unconscionable shortcomings of urban schools, and eventually focused my professional work on education. Working on school reform under the direction of Service Employees International Union (SEIU) president Andy Stern and with many others, we developed a "thin contract," an alternative to complex teacher's union contracts that precluded many reform efforts. Eventually I went on to work for Chancellor Michelle Rhee at DC Public Schools, easily marking the strangest year of my career.

The Obama administration is the focus of part five. When working on the federal level, one finds every communication, persuasion, and management skill is put to the test. It is the ultimate "at scale" experience. I publicly battled with the Catholic bishops over reproductive rights, managed media work over a flood of unaccompanied children entering the

United States over the Mexican border, and routinely interacted with the White House. Robust management lessons are shared in this seven-chapter section, from strategies for addressing low performers, to developing strong internal communications capacity.

And finally, part six is focused on leadership and continued learning. Returning home to Chicago, I found that the lessons kept coming in the form of building a communication shop from scratch at a prestigious research center, to making the best use of new and growing social media channels, to incorporating large-language artificial intelligence models into communication practices. This six-chapter section closes with a guide to developing a robust and evidence-based communication plan, based on many of the experiences shared in this book. A closing chapter puts work and career in the context of family, showing how critical aspects of personal and professional life intersect at potential advantage to both.

Memory is notoriously fallible, so I used it primarily as a starting point. Where newspaper articles and other public information are available, they are cited. My personal journals, which I have kept throughout my life, were also an important, though private, source for this book. During the Obama administration I maintained a digital work diary to ensure a robust record of events that have broader historic implications. And finally I've shared the manuscript with many of the people involved to check for accuracy and have edited based on the nuance they have added.

Since I focus on my working-class background, I would be remiss to not acknowledge my privilege. I am an educated, white American woman who stopped being working class long ago. My privileges are many, from being able to use the bathroom whenever I choose at work, to only needing to clean up after people I love. I am descended from people who had little, but their struggles brought them to a land whose history was defiled by the destruction of Indigenous people and to a country that bore and still suffers from the racism that rationalized slavery. I am grateful to my African American and Native American teachers, people you will meet in these pages. I am hopeful that my communication work has lifted the voices of those who do not have the educational privilege to write and the class privilege to have the time to do so. And I am grateful to you, the reader who will spend time with these stories. I hope my experiences can, in some small way, supplement and inform your own.

Acknowledgments

I am grateful to all of my colleagues over the past four decades. You have been my teachers, my friends, my daytime family. I endlessly appreciate my late parents, Tom and Audrey McMullen, who taught me to enjoy work. I was fortunate to have a few people who gave me opportunities that changed the trajectory of my career. Thank you Andy Stern, Anita Dunn, and George Sheldon for seeing me.

Several talented and diligent friends put many hours into editing this book. Thank you Noreen Willhelm, Vince McKelvey, and Alan Neff. Many others read sections of this book to ensure their accuracy, conscientiously reviewing chapters, long before it was clear this work would be published. I appreciate their valuable time, especially Molly Martin (pseudonym), Mishaela Durán, and Katie Test. And everyone benefits from a solid cheering section that brings the joy. For me that was my DC book group. Thank you Judy Berman, Larra Clark, Deborah James, Kathleen Kilbane, Julie Kruse, and Sherri Moses for being such supportive friends. The captain of this cheering section is the incomparable Margrete Strand Rangnes, whose love and zeal are as inexhaustible as they are uplifting.

Jeff Epton is in a category of his own. He is my first and last editor, critical when he needs to be but always enthusiastic. He lugged multiple boxes of clippings, files, and journals down from storage shelves (and back up again), solved computer problems, endured countless days of me popping out of bed before 5 a.m. to write, and reviewed every word of this book numerous times, each pass making it better. Like all of the best things in my life, it would not have happened without him.

Introduction

With just 18 months left in the Obama administration, a group of senior political appointees at the US Department of Health and Human Services got a special treat: a daylong retreat at Camp David. After boarding a bus on the National Mall at sunrise, we traveled to a mountainous area in Maryland, where we arrived at the massive entry fence to the camp and handed over our personal phones and work Blackberrys to the heavily armed security detail.

We had a day of inspiring talks that challenged us to focus relentlessly on our highest priorities as we closed President Barack Obama's second term. Those of us in external affairs had to practice even greater message discipline as we interacted with the press and state and local officials. And we all had to take strategic steps to embed positive changes so they would outlast the current presidency.

But our day at Camp David wasn't all work. We also got to walk in the woods, bowl, climb, swim, and drink at the Shangri-La bar. I loved the connection to history that I felt that day. Throughout the compound framed photos mark events that took place at Camp David: Dwight Eisenhower's meeting with secretary of the Communist Party of the Soviet Union Nikita Khrushchev in 1959, Jimmy Carter's hosting of Egyptian president Anwar al-Sadat and Israeli prime minister Menachem Begin in 1978, Ronald Reagan's hosting of British prime minister Margaret Thatcher in 1984.[1] The primary function of Camp David, though, was to provide a place where the president and his family could move freely in a secure and private location. Most of the pictures are families playing and eating together, celebrating holidays.

The year I was born, 1960, Dwight Eisenhower and his family were using the camp regularly.[2] By 1963, two years into the Kennedy presidency,
Jacqueline Kennedy moved all of her horses there, and JFK had the navy
personnel who staff Camp David build a pony ring for his six-year-old
daughter, Caroline, and her pony Macaroni.[3]

The Irish Catholic community in Pittsburgh where I was raised
strongly identified with the Kennedys, even though they had a lifestyle
and wealth that we couldn't imagine. My great-grandfather Patrick Mc-
Mullen signed his naturalization papers with an X in 1884.[4] The next
two generations of my family held stable, working-class jobs in the same
neighborhood Patrick had settled in all those years before, with my baby
boomer generation providing the first college graduates. Growing up in
our modest South Hills community, a Shirley Temple movie was as close
as we ever got to seeing a little girl with a pony. But here I was, 52 years
after Caroline got her little pony ring, getting to at least play in the same
sandbox for a day.

Every day, as I practice the profession of communication, I reach back
to an earlier experience. Those experiences might point to a successful
tactic, a reliable approach to campaign planning, or a senseless mistake
to avoid. In workshops I have shared stories of successful communication campaigns and the steps taken to achieve them. With my staff teams
I have retold more painful career episodes, which apparently can be as
riveting for others as scanning the damage after a bad traffic accident.
But every look back, even through a sometimes-gauzy nostalgic filter, provides a clue to a move forward. It's a foundation on which I build and a
foundation on which I have seen my colleagues build in unexpected ways.
With this book, that foundation is yours to work with as well.

As a young journalism student in the late '70s, when even the small-
est cities had daily, printed newspapers, I could not have seen this career
coming. I only saw myself as a reporter. Now, with constant technological
change and the new communication channels they foster, the specifics of
what professional communicators will be doing in 20 years is even more
unpredictable. But we know they will write and speak and need to persuade. It is my hope that the lessons in this book will prove fundamental

enough to endure changes in channels and delivery methods. I'm trying to age well, and I set out to capture stories that will do the same.

Continuing my education, practicing my craft, and following my heart proved a powerful and rewarding career strategy. This one professional journey is the organizing principle for this book, but it's a journey with hundreds of others who taught me, learned with me, and became an important part of my life. Never underestimate the community that you can build and cultivate at work and how much the strength of that community can drive achievement and happiness. You will meet dozens of members of that community in the following pages, and you will learn from them, too.

That day at Camp David provided something every work group needs: a time to retreat together without the crush of deadlines and to find motivation in the connection to something larger. Checking our phones at the gate meant we couldn't even be tempted to do work, or even to know what was going on outside the camp. We literally had time to play.

In the middle of the afternoon, I commandeered one of the many golf carts on the grounds to take a little tour around the perimeter of the camp. I pulled up to different colleagues, asking them if they wanted to go for a ride. I started shuttling people around from one place in the camp to another, waving at the guys with big guns. Then I did my last stop at the Shangri-la bar. It was time for cocktail hour before boarding the bus home.

It was a good ride. One of many.

Part One

Foundations

1

Learning to Work

I learned how to work from my family. It was what we did together. My mother, Audrey McMullen, ran the house like a project manager for a small business. Maintenance routines were steady and robust. Every Saturday the bottom sheets and the pillowcases were put in the wash, the top sheet moved to the bottom. (No fitted sheets in the 1960s.) It was my job to iron all the pillowcases. Groceries were strategically purchased to make every penny go as far as possible; meals planned well in advance were built around the best prices that week.

My sister, 11 years my senior, and I were responsible for most domestic tasks, while my three older brothers were charged with lawn and car maintenance. Even friends who slept over, much to their surprise, would get a little list of tasks to accomplish. I grew up thinking everyone woke up to a daily work plan from their mother waiting for them by their breakfast cereal bowl.

The boys all worked at the Pennzoil service station that my dad, Tom McMullen, managed in Dormont, a couple miles from our house. In the early '70s, my mom and I talked my dad into letting me work there, too. At the time, service stations were hiring women to pump gas, having them wear short shorts to attract customers. My dad was horrified at the notion that my employment there would put me on display, so my duties were strictly behind the scenes. I would use a giant stick to measure the gas left in the tanks at the end of the day, fill vending machines with orange pop and cream soda, clean the bathrooms, wash the windows, and, eventually, keep the books.

Most important, though, I was there enough to learn from my father's family-oriented management style. The station was open six days a week, from 8 a.m. to 8 p.m., and those were pretty much his hours. If someone's kid drove their family car into a ditch at two in the morning and the car needed to be pulled out with a tow truck, those were his hours, too. He demanded more of himself than anyone who worked for him, and didn't pay himself very well. Employees came to our house for beer and meals on a regular basis. If a customer was having a hard time—particularly if it was a family where there was no father in the house—they often didn't get a bill.

The service station was an extension of our home. Accordingly, expectations were higher for us kids than they were for the grown men working there. We were the progeny of the proprietor and had to interact with the public accordingly.

When I was a senior in high school, in 1978, Pennzoil decided to close their service stations, converting them all to convenience stores. They gave my dad a job driving an oil truck, delivering oil to businesses within a couple hours of Pittsburgh. It was Dad's first union job; he joined the Teamsters. He was done with work by 4 p.m.—the shortest workday of his life. But he was always meticulous about his vehicles, so frequently, he'd stick around and wash and polish his truck after his shift. The union guys would tell him that he shouldn't be doing that off the clock. He'd just smile and keep washing his truck, always after he clocked out.

While Dad was transitioning from service station manager to truck-driving employee, Mom was taking her own big work step. A federal program designed to help low-income people get better jobs, the Comprehensive Employment and Training Act (CETA), made it possible for Mom to become a licensed practical nurse. Her tuition, books, and uniforms were paid for, and she was paid a modest wage to attend. Then in her 50s, Mom would soon have her first job with decent pay, full benefits, and reasonable hours. And she got to run circles around the charge nurses as she applied her management skills at the senior care facilities where she worked.

As my parents were shifting into the last phase of their working life, I, their fifth and youngest child, was leaving for West Virginia University (WVU) to study journalism. Going from working-class Pittsburgh to college at WVU was a minimal culture shift. At that time, the large majority of WVU students were first-generation college students. Roughly half of the first-year girls on my dorm floor were from Pittsburgh. We talked the same, wore similar clothes, and listened to the same music, and we all drank, swore, and smoked too much.

West Virginia is where my professional journey, and lessons, began. Through early reporting at community and university publications, I learned the power of the coal industry, over the state, the land, and my school. Reporting took me onto the Akwesasne Mohawk Reservation in upstate New York and behind the Iron Curtain in the Soviet Union. Through these and other experiences, I came to understand the timidity and caution of so many media outlets and the ideological and practical limitations of the mainstream media. Moving into nonprofit communications, I learned the importance of careful audience analysis and messaging strategy to achieve persuasion and, ultimately, change.

This first phase of my career also laid the groundwork for managerial roles. No course prepared me for that; my parents did. My father never read anything but the daily newspaper, but he would have been a prime case study for the *Harvard Business Review*, which frequently writes about the importance of building community at work and about creating an atmosphere where others can bring their whole and true selves to the job. My mother never trained to be a project manager, but she could see the order and specifics of the many small tasks that needed to be done to accomplish a larger goal, and she delegated accordingly.

Most important, though, I grew up working with people I loved and with the idea that you should love the people you work with.

LESSON LEARNED

Our relationship to work starts early. Early lessons about how to work with others to accomplish a shared goal can last a career.

2

The Cost of Coal

My first days as a journalist were in an old wood-frame house perched on a hill above Morgantown, West Virginia. The house held the offices of the *Mountain Journal*, a monthly tabloid ably edited by Martin Berg and published by the nonprofit Mountain Community Union. At 19, I attended my first editorial meeting in the sparsely furnished first-floor living room, most of us sitting in folding chairs or on the threadbare rug. There we would decide on stories and who would write what.

Coal was at the center of life and culture in West Virginia, and it was at the center of our editorial content. Coke plants, black lung, brown lung, conferences of mine workers, public policy developments related to worker safety—those were the stories that filled our pages.

One of the more unusual coal-related stories was the development of "solvent refined coal." SRC, as it was known, was an effort to give new life to dirty, low-grade coal. It was a process by which coal was pulverized, mixed with a solvent, cooked at high temperatures, filtered, and ultimately turned into a liquid fuel source. For the oil and gas industry it was a way to create a new kind of oil. In reality, the industry was creating a toxic substance that could threaten the life of any worker who came into contact with it, and it could cause widespread environmental devastation in the event of a major spill or plant accident.

In July 1980, just a couple weeks before my 20th birthday, I interviewed a spokesperson from Gulf Oil about their proposed Solvent Refined Coal (SRC 2) plant to be built in Fort Martin, West Virginia. In the interview, I mentioned the public suspicion that Gulf Oil wasn't telling us everything they knew about this proposed plant or the operations at the first-ever SRC plant in Fort Lewis, Washington. He dismissed the question, labeling it "conspiracy paranoia" rooted in the general cynicism of modern society.[1]

The day after my interview, on July 30, the Monongahela Alliance for Community Protection reported that a spill of 2,300 gallons of extremely hazardous material had occurred at the Fort Lewis plant. The organization also uncovered three other accidents at the same plant in the preceding months. Most disturbing was that the environmental impact statement released by the US Department of Energy on the West Virginia plant did not mention the spill, even though the report was published five months after the incident.

It was a powerful lesson early in my journalistic career. Like many in journalism school in the late '70s and early '80s, I was inspired by the role that journalists played in releasing the Pentagon Papers and uncovering the Watergate conspiracy in the early 1970s. Perhaps at no time in our history were journalists seen as more important. They were the tough, smart, pen-mightier-than-the-sword heroes of democracy. That's what I wanted to be.

In England's 1871 census, my paternal great-grandfather Patrick McMullen was listed as a "driver" in the coal mines in Durham. A driver, or pony driver more precisely, leads the horses hauling carts of coal through the underground roads and then up to the surface. He was 13 years old. Not long after that, his parents and six siblings emigrated to America, where work in coal mines continued in southwestern Pennsylvania.

Signing his naturalization papers with an X, Patrick became a US citizen in 1884 at the age of 26.[2] One year later, my grandfather Hugh was born. By 1920 census records show Hugh to be age 34, the father of four, and living on McMonagle Avenue in Pittsburgh. His occupation: "employee—coal mine."[3]

Miners also appeared in maternal branches of my family, from France and Germany. Coal miners up every family tree. I knew little of this when I chose to go to journalism school at West Virginia University. In retrospect, though, I realized how lucky I was to cover and challenge the coal industry rather than dig, haul, and breathe the stuff. And I was proud to in some way be part of the coal lineage, perhaps even working to correct past wrongs, or at least prevent future ones.

In 1980, a century after my great-grandfather was a child worker in coal mines in England, Gulf Oil said that future solvent refined coal workers would be protected from the toxic material they were processing. All they had to do was shower at the plant before and after each shift, do a complete change of clothing—from underwear to boots—after arrival and before departure, and apply protective cream to their hands several times a day. In the areas where there is a higher potential for accidental contact with process materials, workers would have to wear liquid-resistant suits with face shields.

These measures represented the "much more sophisticated" approach compared to an earlier coal liquefaction plant in Institute, West Virginia, in the 1950s, where 50 percent of the workers got skin cancer or developed precancerous lesions.[4]

These details and many others were hashed out in public hearings from July through December 1980. Protests got louder. While the Department of Energy produced a sanitized environmental impact statement, that statement was not accepted by the Environmental Protection Agency. (Score one for federal agency checks and balances.)

On December 11, I wrote an editorial in the *Daily Athenaeum*, the student newspaper, blasting West Virginia University for silencing its academic critics of the plant.[5] "As a reporter I had been covering this issue for over six months, and I had consistently run up against unquotable sources," I wrote. "Why couldn't they be quoted? Their reason: Because of their affiliation with the University. This of course should not be the case. But it has been."

The editorial was in response to public statements from the university's vice president of energy mineral resources assuring participants in a public event that the university is and would remain steadfastly neutral on the plant. But the university was poised to gain millions in research grants related to coal liquefaction, and it was as entwined with the coal industry as was any other West Virginia institution. If Morgantown wasn't exactly a company town, West Virginia was a company state.

It was the only piece I wrote in my four years at that paper that resulted in a call from the provost to our general manager, Brentz F. Thompson, a kindly retired journalist who was the resident adult in the room at the student-run newspaper. I showed him my documentation of all the university experts who wouldn't be quoted. Thompson's response: "carry on."

That same week, the Monongahela Alliance for Community Protection filed suit against the Monongalia County Development Authority on the grounds that it had violated the West Virginia Freedom of Information Act. The suit demanded records of all decisions of the executive committee, detailed financial reports, and any agreements between the development authority and any corporation related to the SRC project. Within weeks, the court ruled in the alliance's favor.

By January of 1981 the plans for the plant were starting to crumble. Germany and Japan had previously contracted with the United States to finance half of the plant in return for the technology that would be developed during the plant's planning and operation phases. But then Germany announced that it would reduce or cancel its more than $300 million share of the $1.4 billion project. A local man owned 700 acres of the land that was to be used as a slag disposal area for the plant. He decided to pull out of the project.

In late February university faculty participated in a public colloquium on synfuels development. This gave the political science faculty and other more critical members of the faculty an opportunity to challenge the coal-leaning mineral resources faculty. It also gave many audience participants the opportunity to point out how ridiculous it would be to try something this dangerous and expensive when we could be investing in renewable resources like solar.

Now, in 2022, when you search the internet for "solvent refined coal," you only get news articles and government reports from this time around 1980. It was a far-fetched effort driven not by a desire for alternative energy sources but by a desire to continue to make money from a limited, nonrenewable, dirty resource and to do so by sacrificing the health of a poor and desperate workforce. It's been the story of coal, and of West Virginia, for literally hundreds of years. Sen. Joe Manchin (D-WV) recently carried on this tradition with a one-man blockade of 2022's most important green energy legislation.

We know better now. Coal is dirty, dangerous, and finite. There are better ways to produce energy, and there are certainly better jobs to create. We also know that the energy industry's influence on government

and other institutions is disproportionate and dangerous. An independent media, along with community activists, are a necessary check on
this power.

LESSON LEARNED

Resistance to truth is frequently in direct proportion to the amount of
money at stake. Rely on sources who stand outside the circle of financial
benefit.

3

A Native Challenge

If President Jimmy Carter hadn't reintroduced the draft in January of 1980, I wouldn't have been shivering in an outhouse on the Akwesasne Mohawk Reservation on the New York–Canada border 15 months later.

As a 19-year-old student at West Virginia University, I was passionately against the draft. Everything I was learning about US foreign policy—from why the American hostages were taken in Iran to whom the US supported in Central America—was appalling to me. And a case was coming before the Supreme Court that could eliminate the gender restriction for selective service; a draft for women felt imminent. I couldn't stomach the idea of serving in the military to carry out a morally bankrupt foreign policy.

In the summer of 1980, as an activist in the Committee Against Registration and the Draft at WVU, I was asked to speak on a panel at an antidraft event held in the student union. It was my first public-speaking event, and a letter home reflected how proud I was to couch my arguments in a patriotic way, referring to principles of the "founding fathers." While my politics were veering further left, I still craved the approval of my World War II–era parents.

After the panel, a tall, husky young man with long, wavy black hair approached me. He wanted to talk to me about the founding fathers and their principles. A few years older than me, he was gentle but direct. He said he was Native American and that his people were still in direct conflict with the US government. He said our country's foundations were anything but principled.

His name was Ray Cook. Just weeks before he and other Mohawk traditionalists waited, armed, as New York state troopers massed at the Racquette Point Road entrance to the Akwesasne Reservation, also called the

St. Regis Reservation, which straddles the border between Canada and the United States along the Saint Lawrence River. Eventually, the troopers fell back, but they had identified and issued indictments to many of the Nation members involved, including Ray. They dispersed, and Ray ended up in Morgantown, West Virginia, of all places.

But I didn't know any of that, then. I just thought he had a point. And I was incredibly grateful that he spoke to me directly afterward instead of challenging me in front of an audience. So I invited him to come with the panelists and others in the antidraft organization to the bar we frequented, Maxwell's on High Street. He joined us and for a short period that summer, Ray became part of our small dissident community. He had served in Beirut as a US marine from 1975 to 1977; he brought a maturity from experience that set him apart, even though he was only 23. Eventually, things cooled off at Akwesasne and he returned to the reservation, where he lived with his wife, Neddie.

I stayed in touch with Ray through letters. I wanted to visit the reservation and learn more about the Mohawk Nation and its current conflict with the US government. I thought the sovereignty struggles and armed conflict Ray was talking about were ancient history, but they were clearly a current story.

At this point in my life I was grocery shopping with a calculator so that I was sure I wouldn't spend more money than I had. Travel money was out of the question. But I applied to a National Geographic fund for student journalists to pursue specific projects. I wrote up a proposal with a budget that included Greyhound bus fare (flying wouldn't have occurred to me), a few other expenses, and a commitment to publish a piece in the student newspaper, the *Daily Athenaeum*. I won the small grant and made plans to visit the Akwesasne Nation on my spring break.

In April of 1981 I boarded a Greyhound bus to Syracuse, New York, where I spent the night in a rundown YMCA. The next day I took a bus to Hogansburg, New York, where Ray and Neddie picked me up and took me back to their home on the reservation—a garage where they lived in a small, two-room space on the second floor. There was a roaring woodstove but no electricity and no running water.

With Ray as my guide, I had access to Tribal leaders in their own homes and in the community center, a large space where fry bread was always available and bingo was the regular community activity.

"America is not a democracy, because there is one person at the head of it," Bear Clan chief Loran Thompson said to me, sitting at a large table in that community center. "Each of our clans has three chiefs, nine altogether in the Mohawk Nation, representing the bear, the wolf, and the turtle clans. The chiefs are chosen by clan mothers, who are chosen by the people."

That, he said, is what democracy looks like. Thompson and others in the traditional camp saw all US government aid—from education, to housing, to health care—as a danger to their people. These "gifts" imposed cultural standards, such as promotion of English and eradication of the Mohawk language, and created damaging dependency. This view put them at odds with the Tribal Council, the state-sponsored elective system on the reservation that had a cooperative relationship with the US government and its agencies. It also put them in a distinctly different place from the American left, which supported more comprehensive social safety nets.

"We are put here to make sure that everything is preserved for the future," Thompson continued. "We can't use up or destroy things. We have to take care of them so we can give them to our grandchildren."

On this the Native factions, the traditionals and the Tribal Council, agreed. Every person I spoke with was profoundly affected by the careless approach to natural resources that white people had taken along the Saint Lawrence Seaway. Large plants—Reynolds Metal Corporation, General Motors, Alcoa—punctuated the river landscape with gray boxy structures and looming smokestacks. Each, over the years, had spewed its own specific poisons into the air, land, and water. The Domtar Pulp Mill was responsible for mercury poisoning in the Saint Lawrence River that destroyed much of the reservation's fish supply and got into their water supply.[6] Toxic chemicals and polychlorinated biphenyls (PCBs) also poured into the river from industries and sewer lines all the way upstream to Lake Erie.[7] The genuine independence desired by those on the reservation was routinely undermined by private industry's callous disregard for the natural resources that could sustain that independence.

✉

Learning can be drug-like in its disorientation. Absorbing so much new information is like emerging from a subway stop in a strange city: there is too much to take in to even know where you are, let alone where to go. At Akwesasne I interviewed educators, health-care providers, traditional dance leaders. I also spent a lot of time just hanging out with Ray and his friends. All day, people casually went in and out of each other's houses, like a large extended family. We would walk into a home where Led Zeppelin was playing and a group of young adults who looked an awful lot like my friends back home were smoking pot. We'd join them, and I'd feel quite at home. It would take a dramatic turn in the conversation to remind me that I was in a different country, with a different people.

Akwesasne members were stunningly generous to me. They treated a naive, white student journalist with respect, affording me time for interviews and many long conversations. My sense of shame associated with my race and my country's history grew with each day. Finally, I came to understand the point about founding "principles" that Ray made to me the summer before.

I wish I could thank him. But Ray died in July 2019; he was 62. He had spent his life as a journalist, graduating from Cornell University with a degree in radio and communications.[8] One of his first journalistic ventures was broadcasting live from the siege at Racquette Point in 1980, the event that led to him being on the lam in West Virginia. That was also the beginning of Akwesasne Freedom Radio, which he went back to build out from a garage on the reservation and which eventually became Mohawk Nation Radio. He also wrote for the Indigenous Press Network and owned Rezzdog Associates, a communication consulting firm. He spent his career advocating for veterans and Native Americans.

It's not clear why Raymond J. "Wahnitiio" Cook died so young. His obituary on July 20, 2019, in *Indian Country Today*,[9] referred to various health issues, some related to PTSD, that were exacerbated when he was in a serious car accident in Arizona while on assignment for a story about veterans' health issues. But the wonderfully nonformulaic obituary revealed much about Ray Cook.

"He could be loud, abrasive, even obnoxious, but he was honest," the *Indian Country Today* obituary read. "He called some of these incidents, Man things, Marine things, Dad things. So yeah, loud and opinionated. But in the end, he wanted to see and work toward a better world. And all that is done with love, not hate."

I never saw that more belligerent side of Ray. What I saw was a committed young man who was willing to give me entrée into his world. Like most people of color, he understood the white, American world because it was where he had to live. And, no matter how humble my background, that was my world. But I could only know his world by both initiative and invitation.

The view from there was stunning. I saw the iridescent green clouds of the northern lights for the first time. And I saw my country in a way that would eternally affect my worldview and my journalistic choices. Thank you Ray Cook.

LESSON LEARNED

Listen to those who challenge you, and go to places where you are not comfortable. That is where you will learn the most.

4

The Wrong Journalism Jobs

The same spring that I was at Akwesasne, I was accepted into the American Society of Magazine Editors internship program. About 50 rising college seniors from across the country were selected to spend a summer in New York City, each student matched to a specific magazine. It was my first time in New York, and my first brush with the American elite.

We were asked in advance our top choices for magazine placement. I selected the big news magazines of the day as my first choices—*Time*, *Newsweek*, *US News & World Report*. But I came to learn that only the Ivy League students got those top placements. It didn't matter how much of a hot shot college journalist you were; you didn't get the big magazines unless you were already in the club. Merit might have gotten me into the program, but merit had a ceiling. I was matched to *Ladies' Home Journal*.

We lived in New York University dorms on Washington Square, where we got breakfast and dinner every day except Sunday. It was 1981 and I was paid $250 a week, more than I had ever made. I sent almost all of it home to help cover my school expenses for the next year. I would take food from the cafeteria at breakfast to have for lunch and found the cheapest places to eat on Sunday nights—typically 1-dollar falafel sandwiches or 50-cent tacos.

Fortunately for me, Jan Goodwin was the editor of *Ladies' Home Journal*. She went on to be a renowned journalist and author, focusing on areas of conflict like Afghanistan, Pakistan, Iraq, Iran, and Saudi Arabia and writing about human rights. One of my first interactions with her, though, was an embarrassing one. I pitched her a story idea. I don't recall what it was; I only recall her response: "Isn't that rather esoteric?"

I can only imagine how dumbstruck I must have looked by the question. She probably thought I was hurt by the challenge to my pitch. But I couldn't answer her question, because I had no idea what the word *esoteric* meant.

In the end, what I learned about magazine journalism in New York City is that the work was largely trivial and underpaid in a city where it was hard to get by if you were broke. I thought that career route was my dream; the internship showed me that it wasn't. I remember writing a very high-handed critique of the internship as my final piece of work. I talked about underutilization of staff, like the health and beauty editor, a registered nurse, who spent a week rewriting a paragraph about a specific brand of mascara. I will always be grateful for Jan Goodwin's response to it. I sat in her nice office with the view of midtown Manhattan as she sat and read it. Then she looked up at me and, with a bemused expression, said: "From the mouths of babes."

That summer, I also volunteered in the evenings for a small, New York–based weekly called the *Guardian*. Initially called the *National Guardian*, it was founded in 1948 and was a mainstay of American left-wing publications until it ceased publication in 1992.[10] I proofread galleys before they went to press and successfully pitched an article about the Akwesasne Reservation. I wrote about the conflict with US authorities on the reservation, and the reservation's alignment with the American Indian Movement. But I also wrote about the traditionals' critique of US social programs that they saw as creating dependency among their people. It was central to their approach to reject use of these programs and develop their own independent services, such as for health and education.

As a socialist paper, though, the *Guardian* was unequivocally supportive of government-provided social services. They wanted to cut that part out. I argued that this analysis, and the strategy that emerged from it, was central to one important faction of Native American resistance. They cut it out anyway. That was the last piece I wrote for them.

After I graduated with a journalism degree, I got a job at *Sojourners Magazine* in Washington, DC, in 1982. I knew *Sojourners* as a Christian magazine with a strong commitment to justice in Central America. By then, my first husband and I were active in the Society of Friends, also known as Quakers, and were at home among faith-based activists. The fact that those who ran *Sojourners* magazine were part of an intentional community that took a collective vow of poverty was also okay with us. I agreed to receive subsistence pay, based on my budget. I made $500 a month.

I was to learn, though, that the voluntarily poor at *Sojourners* were the most elite group I had ever yet met. They were the sons and daughters of diplomats, physicians, and corporate executives. Most had gone to Ivy League schools or selective-admission liberal arts colleges. Their vocabularies were awesome; they didn't swear. Their cultural and literary references flew right over my head.

I was, and not for the last time in my career, out of place because of my class background. And I could feel that they thought so too. Over time I came to understand that even left-wing evangelical Christianity was far too conservative for me. But I also felt like I needed to prove myself. My grammatical and editing skills were every bit as good as theirs (thank you Catholic schools) and I had *The Associated Press Stylebook* internalized in a way that none of them did (thank you WVU). They could write with a broader range of words and more flourish than I could but not as quickly or clearly. My writing training was as workmanlike as my background, and that skill set protected me from feeling inferior. I may not have been a cultural fit with them, but I could make a competent contribution to our collective product.

And I was learning from them. No matter how modestly they presented in their thrift store clothes, their manners of speech were refined, their style of interaction was restrained, and their experiences were rich in books read and countries visited. To an outsider, we would have looked the same—educated, well fed, almost completely white first-world people. But my 22-year-old self had a hard time believing that we all had grown up in the same country.

I left these experiences in New York City and Washington, DC, with the power of an immersive experience in a different culture. I was learning the rules of engagement among those with the most privilege. It became clear to me why they thought they were better than me, just as it became clear that they weren't.

LESSON LEARNED

The jobs you think you want may not be right for you. Volunteer, take internships and entry-level positions to try out positions and employers, and keep moving until you find the right fit.

5

Stop the Presses

My first and only daily newspaper job was at the *Palladium-Item* in Richmond, Indiana. After leaving Washington, DC, we had moved to the Midwest for my then-husband, Bruce Arnold, to attend seminary at the Earlham School of Religion in Richmond. He already had his master's in social work from WVU and wanted to supplement his rural social work education with theological training.

The daily newspaper in Richmond, the *Palladium-Item*, was my obvious go-to for work. The *Pal-Item* was one of the last of a dying breed—an afternoon newspaper. Our copy deadlines were typically the night before so that the editing and layout could happen in the morning, and the presses would start to roll by 11 a.m. It was part of the Gannett newspaper chain, and *USA Today* for the entire Midwest market was printed there, giving us the advantage of a state-of-the-art, full-color printing press. We might have been one the best-looking small-town papers in the country.

In 1984 I started in the features department. "A boy and his hog," a story about a local boy with a pet pig who responded to a remarkable number of verbal commands was one of my big stories. And then there was the two-page full-color photo spread of the Rose City parade. On a particularly good day, I got to interview musician Noel Paul Stookey, formerly of Peter, Paul and Mary. (He was lovely.) I was bored out of my mind.

And my boss, the features editor, was an incongruously confident, awkward guy in his mid-30s who once suggested that he, another male colleague, and I get together to watch pornography. I'll never forget what that colleague said in response. "I once saw a stag film at a bachelor party," he said. "After five minutes I wanted to go home and have sex with my wife. After 15 minutes I never wanted to have sex again."

I asked to be moved to the news desk. There were no women editors or reporters on the news side at the time. I got my transfer and was assigned to cover the school system and county government. I soon gained a reputation for fast writing, allowing me to typically do more than one story a day. Unlike many of my male colleagues, I also had the advantage of numerous typing classes required of girls in my high school.

When you work in publishing, you get to experience a unique, collective professional moment: when the publication is put to bed. For years this was when you delivered a box of prepared galleys—pages—to the printshop, where they would make plates for the printing presses. Then it became a digital transmission. But the feeling is the same: you did it, you are done, and you did it together—the skills of dozens of people were applied over 24 hours and you have this tangible thing to show for it: a newspaper. In that moment everyone takes a breath, stretches their legs, grabs a coffee, sometimes mercilessly teasing each other about something that happened working on that edition. (The aforementioned features editor was frequently the butt of jokes. When he was wearing his white pants, this would be when we'd tell him he looked like an ice-cream man and start ordering frozen treats from him.)

That was the kind of moment we were having at the *Pal-Item* at about 10:30 a.m. on January 28, 1986. As frequently happened, we ended up around the big square of desks at the far end of the newsroom, staffed by editors. A large TV overlooked the room, hanging above the news wire machines.

That morning we actually had something to watch: a space shuttle launch. It was the *Challenger*, with the first-ever civilian passenger, Christa McAuliffe, a teacher. As we stood there we felt the familiar rumble through the floor of the building as the printing presses started for that day's run of the *Palladium-Item*.

This was the 25th space shuttle launch; it wasn't as if the whole nation tuned in, or even that those of us watching were particularly riveted. It felt routine, and when parts of the shuttle and launch apparatus seemed to go in different directions, many thought it was just the shuttle breaking away from the rocket booster. But then we realized we were looking at nothing but two white plumes going in different directions with no discernable structure left. *Challenger* was gone. Incinerated.

Everyone—the NASA announcer, the CNN host, people on the

ground watching the launch, those of us in the *Pal-Item* newsroom—held our collective breath for what felt like minutes. "Flight controllers looking very carefully at the situation," we heard the NASA operator say. "Obviously a major malfunction. . . . We have no downlink."[11] We could still feel the presses rumbling when the city editor, John Harmon, leapt across the newsroom heading for the corner door to the press room, yelling as he ran: "Stop the presses!"

I had only one previous experience of pulling back and rebuilding a front page. Four years before, on December 8, 1980, I was working as the production director at the *Daily Athenaeum*, the WVU student newspaper. We were boxing up the galleys at around 11 p.m. when news came over the wire that John Lennon had been shot. We unboxed the galleys, added the news about Lennon's death, and had a late and sad night.[12]

At the *Palladium-Item* the presses stopped. The original of the front page was brought back into the production department, and the layout staff started dismantling and rebuilding the page.

We had one wire story in hand that covered the reasons the launch had been delayed—a faulty gage and then icicles on the launch pad. The editors set to writing a new headline, awaiting an updated story from the Associated Press. Years before the World Wide Web and even fax machines, we huddled around the wire, waiting for a photo of the crew to slowly crank through the machine.

After what felt like an interminable time, the relay was complete and ripped off the machine. "Give it to McMullen," said the gruff but capable Harmon. It was the closest he would ever come to complimenting me. I quickly wrote a long caption for the photo of four beaming crew members as they walked to the shuttle just hours before:

> The crew of the Space Shuttle 51-L walks from their quarters en route to the Space Shuttle orbiter Challenger early Tuesday morning. The shuttle exploded seconds after takeoff. No survivors were found as of press time. Crew members are, left to right, Ellison Onizuka, Greg Jarvis, Christa McAuliffe and Mike Smith.[13]

In addition to being the first civilian on a shuttle, crew member Judy Resnik was the second woman US astronaut who had been in space, crew member Ronald McNair the second African American.

The text was sent to the editing desk and then to layout. An AP story came through from the White House, reporting that President Ronald Reagan was in a meeting with his staff to prepare for that night's State of the Union address when news came in about the shuttle. The page was reset, and within 30 minutes the presses were rolling once more.

The same day as the shuttle explosion, Ford Motor Company had announced a new production line at a local plant. The line was to produce condensers for their 1988 vehicles, and management credited a recent "two-tier" agreement with the union as the reason for their success. I'm sure Ford was hoping for much bigger play for this story, which frames their practice of lower pay and benefits for the next generation of workers as key to their success. But this big story became very small after the shuttle disaster.

When organizations work to use the mass media to communicate with a broader audience, they are always competing with the most compelling news of the day. On the opinion pages they are competing with paid full-time writers and prominent experts. Even if their story is not cut, bumped by breaking news, it could get considerably less attention because of that news.

Mass media has the potential to be a powerful channel, particularly if you are trying to reach influencers, but it is a channel over which you, ultimately, have no control.

LESSON LEARNED

Mass media is an important but unpredictable tactic in communication campaigns. Plan for media coverage, but don't depend on it. Even those who work there don't know what story will dominate until press time.

6

Reporting behind the Iron Curtain

Some of the best views of Moscow can only be seen from its river. We were taking in that view in one of the first official activities of the US-Soviet citizen diplomacy tour that I was covering in July 1986. On the boat tour we wound past central Moscow, taking in the Byzantine architecture with its elaborate stonework and flamboyant onion domes. We cruised by the imposing red brick Kremlin Walls, with gold-topped cathedrals dotting the horizon behind it.

At 26 I had never left my home country, never had a passport, never gone where people spoke a different language, let alone used a different alphabet. I was ecstatic. Long interested in Russia and its history, I found getting behind the Iron Curtain only added to the allure. Back in Richmond, Indiana, two of my sources on the education beat—a professor at Earlham College and an administrator in Richmond Public Schools—had organized and led the tour.

As I stood on the deck of the tour boat, an American with years of experience in these diplomacy tours approached me. "I don't want to muddy up your trip with this if you aren't interested," Christine Dull, a longtime peace activist, said as we leaned against the ship's rail and looked out over Moscow. "But we have a network of dissidents with whom we are in contact and they appreciate meeting with people from outside the Soviet Union. Since you're working as a journalist on this trip, I thought you might like to talk to them."

She gave me a piece of paper with handwritten names and addresses of people in Moscow, Minsk, and Leningrad. There were a few phone numbers, but mostly addresses. If I wanted to talk to them, I had to get to them. There were, of course, no cell phones, no internet, no Google Maps, no car, no guide. Just addresses—of people who were actively resisting the Soviet government.

That handwritten list transformed my trip.

Two days after we first arrived in Moscow, I gathered up the courage to slip away from the tour and our Soviet minders and set about finding the first person on my list of dissidents. I confided in one person on the tour, a physician I had befriended, about what I was doing and where I was going. I told him to tell the tour guide I wasn't feeling well and was going to stay in my room. I descended into the Moscow subway system, which was quite spectacular with its intricately tiled walls. In the months before the trip, I had studied the Cyrillic alphabet and by the time I landed in Moscow I could at least sound out every letter and (badly) pronounce Russian words. I deployed my minimal Cyrillic skills to figure out the right train to get on to reach the specific outskirts of Moscow where Dr. Yuri Medvedkov lived with his wife, Olga.

After a long train ride, I arrived at the stop. I came up from the station to find myself in a wide-open, desolate-looking land dotted with huge, blocky apartment buildings. I had no idea where to go in this utterly alien landscape. A young woman noticed how perplexed, and foreign, I looked and asked if I needed help. "Yes, please," I said in Russian. I showed her the first part of the address without revealing all of the information. It turned out she was a teacher from Siberia who was visiting family in Moscow and that she spoke English. She was able to get me to the right building, after which I slogged up seven or eight flights of stairs to get to the apartment.

I was looking for a couple, Yuri and Olga, who were both active in a peace group that had been in touch with US activists. I hadn't called, because there was no phone. I knocked, and a tired-looking middle-aged man answered the door. I introduced myself, and he immediately invited me in and set to making tea.

Yuri looked tired for a reason. He had just been released the day before from a Moscow jail. He had been arrested for participating in the Group to Establish Trust Between the U.S. and the U.S.S.R., an unauthorized peace group. Yuri and Olga were both scientists working in the Soviet Union's Institute of Geography. Yuri enjoyed a level of prestige in his job; he had lived abroad, including in the United States, and had once served as the chief ecologist of the World Health Organization.

But with Yuri's and Olga's participation in the Trust Group, their careers suffered. They were demoted and moved to the tiny apartment, where we sat having tea. Both spent time in jail. Their grassroots peace group was critical of the Soviet Union, while the authorized Soviet Peace Group toed the Soviet line that the Soviets could spend resources elsewhere if only the United States was not aggressively invading other nations and building a war machine.

Another member of this peace group was Alexander Tron, a scientist based in Leningrad, now Saint Petersburg. I contacted him the first day we arrived in that city, near the end of our tour. We met that evening and he and I talked for hours—over dinner, walking around the city, and then sitting on the bench near a large fountain. As I sat on that bench, I felt profoundly disoriented. I felt woozy and suddenly worried that I might pass out on the ancient cobblestone pavers around us.

Every meeting with dissidents taught me something I didn't know. Like why I felt so terrible sitting on that park bench. I looked at my watch and saw that it was midnight, even though the sun was still up. I wasn't sick; I was exhausted. I had forgotten about white nights—that at this time of year, this far north in Russia, the sun set after midnight and was up again just a couple hours later. I apologized to Tron, excused myself, went back to the hotel room, and carefully closed the light-blocking shades so that I could sleep through the light.

The stories of these dissidents, and the stark contrast they offered to the information shared in meetings with the state-sanctioned groups, were foundational for the many articles that I wrote on my return. I published pieces in several magazines, and a series of articles in the *Palladium-Item*.

I was no longer employed there, because I had lost my job over this trip. At the *Pal-Item*, I covered education and county government. Both beats were slow over the summer. Since two of my education contacts were leading that summer's citizen diplomacy tour, I thought it would make a great story to cover the trip but knew my little paper couldn't send me. I made an offer: I would pay for my own participation; they just had to give me the time to go and the time to write stories when I returned.

The editor said no way. The only thing I would come back with was Soviet propaganda, he said, and he had no use for it. I disagreed with him, vehemently. I was a trained reporter who would find real stories, in addition to covering the experience of local people on an unusual educational and diplomatic excursion. He would have none of it.

I told him that what his reporters did with their work time was his decision, but what I did with my time was mine. I'm going on the trip, I told him, and quitting this job. I'd be happy to sell him some stories on a freelance basis when I returned. And I did. I sold him stories about the tour, and an op-ed about the pros and cons of life in the Soviet Union. But all those dissident interviews? I went elsewhere with those stories.

Here's the thing: the next summer, the *Pal-Item* sent a reporter on the citizen diplomacy tour. Public sentiment had shifted enough that citizen diplomacy to the Soviet Union had become less fringe. At that time, a decade before the emergence of Fox News, the mainstream media's commitment to centrism was both dispositional and commercial. They so adamantly wanted to look unbiased that they often limited their scope to the center. And they so needed circulation that they overly feared covering topics that would lead to losing groups of readers. "Market driven news operations, like most institutions, resist change," said Charlotte Ryann and Karen Jeffreys in their compelling essay "Challenging Domestic Violence: Trickle-Up Theorizing about Participation and Power in Communication Activism." "Media critics generally concur that US media systems, especially in the second half of the 20th century, have served democracy poorly."[14] These tendencies, and resistance to change, left many mainstream outlets behind the curve on a lot of stories and historic developments.

My editor may not have had confidence I'd go find real stories, but the Soviet authorities certainly noticed what I was up to. I was unaccounted for during too much of the tour. On one of our last short flights in the country, from Minsk back to Moscow, they decided to separate me from the group in the airport. They took me and my luggage into a small, windowless room and proceeded to unpack everything and flip through all my notebooks, where I had been careful to not record any names. Then they separated me from my luggage and put me in an even smaller room and told me to wait.

Enough time had passed that I thought for sure the plane had departed. But I feared that finding a new flight wasn't going to be my biggest problem. Every moment alone in that bare room allowed time to imagine an outcome that ended in a jail cell. Finally, two female security officers came into the room, had me take off my jacket and shoes, and proceeded to do a very thorough and not gentle frisking.

Suddenly, everyone was in a hurry. I was to immediately put my shoes and jacket back on and they returned my suitcase, which was in crazy disarray, and told me to leave. I threw everything together and bolted to the gate, where one member of the tour, my doctor friend, was nervously waiting. Everyone else had boarded; he had volunteered to stay behind. It turned out that the show of force was not to last so long that I would miss my flight.

We rushed outside to the tarmac and up the boarding stairs into the small aircraft. My fellow citizen-diplomats met me with relieved applause. I was safe, almost on my way home, and had an unexpected number of stories to tell.

Profound work experiences can affect your personal life, too. After three weeks of international travel on my own, including a side trip to Northern Ireland to visit family there, I was realizing how much happier I was not being part of a couple. I always remember my Irish cousin Sammy saying to me: "You don't seem like a married person." I'm not sure what he was seeing that led him to say that, but I found myself agreeing with him. My first husband, Bruce, was a good man, but we had met when I was 19 and married when I was 21, long before I knew myself or what I wanted. He was eight years older than me and had a clear vision for his own life and that was to live and work as a rural social worker, counselor, and pastor. After I returned from my international adventure and started a new job in Dayton, Ohio, it became increasingly clear that the life I had with Bruce was not what I wanted.

His commitment to rural social work, though, was to have a permanent effect on my life. When we lived in the small town of West Elkton in southwestern Ohio, where Bruce served as a pastor for a Quaker congregation after he finished seminary, we learned of a family whose six children were not going to school because they didn't have shoes. For their privacy, I will call them the Martin family. We asked members of the church to contribute to help the family. Cash in hand, I went to visit the Martins in my Volkswagen bus and told them I could drive them into the nearest town with a Payless shoe store and get the kids school shoes and gym shoes. To my surprise, the parents told all the girls to get in the van, but neither of them accompanied us. It was the first time I had met them.

Six girls, stairsteps, ages 5 through 12. Three of them redheads like me. Their father, Roy Martin, was in constant trouble with the law, and he and his wife, Mary Lou, struggled to keep the kids clothed and fed. They owned their own small house, and Roy's parents lived in a trailer in the backyard.

Not long after that first meeting, we learned that the family had abandoned the house and moved into a small commercial space that they had access to in nearby Camden. We couldn't imagine why. Eventually, we learned that Roy had been arrested and put the house up for bond, and then he and Mary Lou jumped bond and disappeared. The grandparents fled the property with the kids.

I found out where they were and went to check on them. I told the grandparents that I knew they were taking on an incredible responsibility. I'll get my foster parent license, I said, so that I could be ready to help out when they needed it, particularly with the older girls. At this point, I was speaking only for myself. Bruce and I were no longer a couple, and I soon moved to Dayton.

By that fall I was living in a small rowhouse in the Dayton neighborhood of Five Oaks, where I also worked. Not long after, the two oldest girls—Norah, 15, and Anna, 14—moved in with me.

LESSON LEARNED

Trust yourself, but know what you can afford and manage. Professional risks can lead to new opportunities, and personal commitments can shape your life for decades. Take risks, and make commitments thoughtfully.

7

Friendly Persuasion

Few settings in the United States quite match the intentional austerity of a Quaker meeting house. The symmetry of plain wooden benches and white walls minimize distraction. No interface or iconography is required for spiritual communion among equals who each have "that of God" within them. The only variation in design is the two or three raised facing benches reserved for the elders of the meeting. In many modern meetinghouses, though, even this nod to modest hierarchy is gone and seats are placed in circles or rows facing each other, all on the same level.

The radical nature of the Quaker approach to equality—specifically their insistence that men and women were spiritually equal—was a major driver of their exodus from England to the United States in the 17th century. Through their leadership in the abolitionist movement, criminal justice reform, and the right to conscientious objection to participation in war, Quakers continued to make a distinctive and progressive mark on this country.

In the 1970s, once again ahead of their time, Quakers continued to stir the pot with their insistence on equality—this time creating controversy within their own community. The American Friends Service Committee (AFSC) is a Quaker service organization that began during World War I to provide relief to civilian communities affected by that war. In 1978, AFSC's Board of Directors passed an affirmative action policy that included people of color, people with disabilities—and gays and lesbians. In practice, that meant a detailed set of steps not only in hiring staff but also in personnel policies, including providing domestic partner coverage even though same-sex marriage was illegal at the time.

AFSC was still struggling with internal Quaker constituencies over these gay-affirming policies when I began working there in 1986. After my post-Soviet-trip departure from the *Palladium-Item*, I took a job in AFSC's Dayton, Ohio, office. I produced a newspaper for them, the *Peace and Justice Journal*, meant to communicate about their local work throughout the Midwest.

It became clear, though, that issues between AFSC and key internal stakeholders were an ongoing distraction. Quakers continued to express concern over AFSC's gay-affirming policies. The affirmative action policy had been successful: AFSC staff was indeed diverse. But staff perception that Quakers opposed this policy diminished morale. Staff felt that Quakers opposed *them* as products of this policy, and they resented it.

I had begun taking graduate courses in communication at the University of Dayton after I started at AFSC. My undergraduate degree had prepared me to be a journalist, but it had not prepared me for a broader communication role. As a journalist I had to know how to prepare content for one channel; as a communicator I needed to understand the complete communication process. Central to that process was the audience. If you didn't understand them, your messages weren't going to land and persuade. As AFSC became my lab in graduate school, the first step in the Persuasion Matrix (see figure 1) began to take shape: specifically defining who the audience is for your message.

I proposed an AFSC communication campaign with Quakers, starting with research on just what their concerns were. The Quaker audience is not homogenous; their concerns vary, and the consequences of their disaffection depend on their engagement with and support of the organization.

Geographic divisions of Quakers have annual "yearly meetings," where hundreds of members gather in modest, camp-like environments for several days. I visited every major yearly meeting in the Midwest over the summer of 1988 to catalogue their concerns with AFSC. Quakers are split into three branches: conservative, who dressed "plainly," used "thee and thou," and adhered to historic Christian-centered traditions of Quakerism; Friends United Meeting (FUM), who more closely resembled traditional protestant churches with paid pastors and programmed worship; and Friends General Conference (FGC), the most liberal branch, who had

Figure 1: The Persuasion Matrix

unprogrammed meetings, no paid church leadership, and tended toward active social justice engagement. Table 1 shows the six yearly meetings I visited, tracking the concerns people raised at the session either in a public discussion or one-on-one with me or other representatives of AFSC.

Quakers broke into separate branches for a reason, and those are manifest in this table. Friends General Conference members were the most supportive of and engaged with AFSC. Their concerns were distinct—too little Quaker involvement in the organization. They were totally fine with stands that were pro-gay and -lesbian, and weren't concerned about religious orthodoxy.

Political campaigns have a lot to teach organizations about communications. When you are working to elect a candidate, you have to be clear on who your base supporters are. Then you have to be sure to communicate

Table 1: Quaker Concerns with AFSC, by Branch of Quakerism

Branch	Quaker Body	Major Area of Concern with AFSC		
		Too little Quaker involvement	Gay affirming	Not Christ-centered enough
Conservative	Ohio Yearly Meeting, Conservative		X	X
Friends United Meeting	Indiana Yearly Meeting		X	
	Western Yearly Meeting		X	
Friends General Conference	Illinois Yearly Meeting	X		
	Lake Erie Yearly Meeting	X		
	Ohio Valley Yearly Meeting	X		

with them, maintain their support, ensure their loyalty and mobilization. Campaigns are equally clear on the people whose support they will never get, and so they don't mobilize their limited communication resources to communicate with them.

Members of the Friends General Conference were clearly AFSC's "base." We needed to attend to their distinct and specific concerns. Over the next couple years, we did several workshops where staff of different faiths—Jewish, Catholic, Baptist—discussed the spiritual basis for their social activism. Given FGC members' broad notions of spirituality, this reinforced their notion of AFSC as a faith-based institution. We also emphasized the all-Quaker membership of the Board of Directors, and the requirement that the executive director be a member of the Society of Friends.

We didn't ignore the concerns from the more conservative branches. We launched a series of "worship sharing" sessions focused on gay and lesbian issues. In worship sharing, attendees sit in silence, and individuals speak out as they are moved to do so. The ground rules for these sessions were to speak only from personal experience and to not comment on or judge others' experiences. The Quaker belief that "everyone holds a piece of the truth" was central to this approach.

The sharing in these sessions ranged from one lesbian woman talking about the pain of being rejected by her family, to a man talking about his commitment to the scriptures and to a traditional interpretation of Christianity. Many in the group later talked about hearing some experiences and perspectives for the first time. We didn't think that opinions were changed by the discussion, but we did conclude that there was less hostility and tension around the topic after the two sides had a more personal exposure to and understanding of the other. Postevent evaluations of the workshop were positive, regardless of the participants' perspectives on the issue. From our postvantage of favoring marriage equality today, we know that similar consciousness raising was happening across the country at this same time and for the next couple decades, based largely on highly personal interactions.

Identifying key concerns of an organization's constituencies is a critical step in effective, strategic communications. In professional parlance, this is called "issues detection." When done well and routinely, issues can be identified before they become problematic or even public. But done at any point, taking the time to identify your constituencies in detail and determine their key concerns allows you to attend to them respectfully and effectively. And it allows you to better answer the next questions in the Persuasion Matrix: Why would they take, or not take, your desired action? What messages best address those reasons? Who are the most persuasive messengers to deliver them? It positions you to persuade that audience.

In 1989, largely motivated by the need to put my two foster daughters in separate bedrooms, I also bought a three-bedroom house in the Five Oaks neighborhood, just north of downtown Dayton and a short walk to the AFSC office. Jeff Epton, who was on the Michigan area staff of AFSC, was increasingly becoming part of our household on weekends. When one of the girls would come up missing, which wasn't unusual, he would join me in tracking her down and getting her home. It was an odd courtship period, but it was how we started our family.

My work at AFSC started expanding to include media monitoring and activism, which overlapped with my graduate studies in communications at the University of Dayton. I conducted studies on how few female voices there were in our local paper, the *Dayton Daily News*, and on the high level of errors in local television news. A group of us started an alternative newsletter to fill in a few local coverage holes, which we did for several years. Increasingly, though, that newsletter wasn't enough.

We looked to other cities, which all seemed to have at least one and sometimes competing alternative newsweeklies. Why couldn't we have an alternative newsweekly in Dayton? The business plan research and writing began for what was to become the *Dayton Voice*.

I was 31 and felt very clear on what I needed to do: to be with Jeff and to stay in the Dayton area until the Martin girls were grown. I was not going to be another adult who abandoned them. In 1991, three years after we started seeing each other, Jeff moved to Dayton and we were married.

Jeff and I worked with a group of other activists to complete the business plan for the *Dayton Voice*, and we started raising money to get the venture off the ground. Our tumultuous decade of business ownership and foster parenting in an impoverished, crack-riddled city was about to begin. It would take another decade to recover from the choices we were making in the early '90s. But the adventure was priceless.

LESSON LEARNED

Define your audiences as specifically as possible, understanding which segments are most important to the success of your organization. Know which messages most resonate with them, and engage and communicate with them accordingly.

Part Two

The *Dayton Voice*

8

Watchdogs

Ben Kirby pulled a large knife from its leather sheath and held it within inches of my face. The knife, explained the director of pupil personnel for Dayton Public Schools, was brought to school by an elementary student. A kindergartner, he added, brought a loaded .38 to show-and-tell. These incidents accounted for two of thousands of suspensions in 1993 at Dayton Public Schools (DPS).

Kirby's attempts to intimidate me were blatant. I was working on a story for the *Dayton Voice* about how often Dayton Public Schools kicked students out of school, and he wasn't happy about it. To him, I was a naive, young journalist who didn't understand that the city's public schools were a scary place filled with threatening students, and suspension was one of the few defensive tools available. At this point, though, I had already spent nearly five years as a foster parent in the system, watching my foster daughters of high school age get suspended for behaviors that posed no danger to anyone. And in 1993, 82 of the 5,289 removals were kindergartners and first graders. If a school can't handle five- and six-year-olds, those running it are in the wrong line of work.

I spent days sitting at a table outside of Kirby's office looking through stacks of computer printouts that documented removals of children from Dayton Public Schools. When a school formally suspends a student, due process is required: The school has to notify the parents and students of the reason for suspension; students have a right to a hearing and to appeal the removal. By federal law, the schools also must report suspensions to the US Department of Education, including the child's age, race, and gender. To get around these requirements, DPS created another category: emergency removals. As a result, the only way to know how many kids were removed from school was to look through each school's records as reflected in these computer printouts. If the emergency removals were tabulated anywhere, they weren't showing that data to me. I know Kirby didn't expect me to sit there day after day with a calculator and notepad, adding up each school's removals. But I did just that, and it really pissed him off.

When my calculations were done, I found that only 36 percent of the total removals were formal suspensions, rendering their official suspension figures meaningless.[1] In one year, 20 percent of ninth graders were suspended or removed. That's one-fifth of the students in one of the most critical years in determining if a child will drop out of school. This was in a majority-Black, majority-impoverished school system. Exactly the sort of place where public systems can get away with failing those they are supposed to serve.

Jeff and I had started publishing the alternative newsweekly the *Dayton Voice* in August 1993. Faxing still felt miraculous; the internet was nascent; *Pulp Fiction* and *The Shawshank Redemption* were about to be released. We were to get our first email address. (For the office, of course. Why would we need more than one? It was an *address*.)

We both knew (and know) how flawed public institutions can be. Jeff had served three terms as a city councilman in Ann Arbor, and I was later to go into federal service. It was and is clear that journalism can't fix government but is one of the most powerful channels through which messages are delivered. In the Persuasion Matrix, determining the messengers and channels is a final part of strategic communication planning. While some communication campaigns require quiet, more-direct message delivery, media exposure can create urgency and drive change unlike any other channel. That makes the watchdog role of the press critical. The *Dayton Voice* was born to play this role. We spent precious hours of our limited staff time on investigatory work.

We routinely took on the school system, the police department, and city government. One of our early investigations was of the Montgomery County Community Action Agency (MCCAA)—an antipoverty agency that was grossly misusing funds. Community action agencies were the type of organization that we would typically champion. They provided services, like Head Start preschool and home weatherization, for low-income people.

But under the leadership of David Hernandez, MCCAA was transformed into a personal fiefdom. Federal funds were used to settle race and sex discrimination lawsuits, and contracts were awarded with no competing bids. Credit card bills were chock full of restaurant and hotel charges, including rooms at the Tropicana in Las Vegas. Purchases at jewelry stores were called "employee awards." Equipment was purchased for staff who weren't on the payroll at the time, and home renovations were done where residents did not qualify for any assistance. Employees were pressured to contribute to the MCCAA Political Action Committee through payroll deductions, and federal training and technical assistance funds were used to purchase MCCAA fundraising banquet tickets.

Whistleblowers within MCCAA had been trying to get local media attention for years. The politically powerful and connected Hernandez wrote them all off as disgruntled employees, and the media acquiesced. But a Columbus-based private investigator and editor of the *Ohio Observer*, Marty Yant, pursued the story, and the evidence that he uncovered after a year of probing was incontrovertible. We published his initial findings,[2] and continued covering the story. In February 1995, a month after our first story was published, David Hernandez was put on indefinite leave.

Weeks later, we released a story that Raleigh Trammell, head of the local chapter of the Southern Christian Leadership Conference (SCLC), was both in on and a beneficiary of MCCAA corruption: MCCAA funds were used to rehab and renovate a house that he owned.[3] It was years before Trammell would be held to account. Almost two decades later, in 2011, Trammell was indicted by a Montgomery County grand jury on 51 felony charges, including grand theft, forgery, and tampering with government records. Trammell was stealing the money that that SCLC was receiving to feed low-income elderly people. At the age of 74, he was sentenced to 18 months in prison.

About a month after the MCCAA investigation was published, and after Hernandez was ousted, I remember the investigator, Marty Yant, coming into the office. "So how does that notch in your belt feel?" he asked. I smiled, I'm sure, but was noncommittal. It didn't feel like a notch in my belt. All of our key sources for the story were African American, and the people being ripped off were poor Blacks and Appalachians. Still. Taking down leaders of color didn't make us feel like champions. But the word spread that we were willing to listen to sources for news that mainstream outlets had ignored. That brought more people to our door. Including Ruby Mays.

While Dayton was 45 percent African American, its police force was only 10 percent Black. That disproportionality had both causes and consequences that were frequent subjects of our stories at the *Voice*. Jeff cultivated a stable of sources who worked in the police force and were victims of its excess. What we lacked in investigatory budget, we made up for in forming trusting relationships with people who were in a position to know things.

Ruby Mays was one of those people. She was married to Dr. Dewey Mays, who, in an investigation that was a holdover from the antiwelfare '80s, the Dayton Police Department aggressively pursued for Medicaid fraud. His office was raided with no probable cause, and years of police harassment destroyed his practice.[4] No wrongdoing was ever substantiated.

Jeff's thorough coverage of the harassment of Dr. Mays continued after Dr. Mays died of a stroke that he suffered just days after his office was raided, his files were confiscated, and his practice was closed down.[5] The stories did not, could not, provide justice. They could only provide some vindication for the family.

Within the Dayton Police Department, Jeff also closely followed the case of Lt. David Sherrer, a Black officer who was fired, ostensibly, for lying in an internal investigation.[6] The main difference between Sherrer and the other officers targeted in the investigation was not any detail in his account but that he was Black and all of the other officers were white. As we looked into this story, we found that a Black officer was almost five times more likely to be investigated, disciplined, or fired than a white officer.

Sherrer was fired in April 1997 but returned to duty in September after a ruling by the Civil Service Board. Two years later, the city was apologizing to David Sherrer and awarding him a $75,000 payment after Sherrer won a civil rights complaint against the city. While he wasn't permitted to talk about the negotiations on the settlement, it was clear that he gave up a considerable amount in compensatory damages to get that public apology.

⊠

Every day, African Americans live with and under broken systems, one of the most egregious being police departments. As a white woman, I have been spared not only police brutality but also the shortcomings of other systems that have failed so many. I grew up in the 1960s and 1970s in Pittsburgh, when all Catholic kids were able to go to Catholic schools, regardless of their economic means. Some of us had to do things like clean locker rooms on weekends to be there, but we had access to a good education and committed teachers.

In 1988, 10 years after I graduated from high school, Anna, my 15-year-old foster daughter, was attending Dayton Public Schools. She came home one day with an English homework sheet that required her to fill in the names of 10 brands of tennis shoes. It would have been a ridiculous assignment at any age but was appalling for a sophomore in high school. I was reading and discussing *The Bell Jar* by Sylvia Plath at that age. The disparity between our educational experiences was alarming and revealing: no way kids at her high school had the same shot at success as the kids at mine.

This same foster daughter with the lousy English assignment would get in trouble for skipping school. Anna's punishment? Suspension. "It's one thing to have a punishment fit the crime; it's another to have it duplicate it." Paul Smith of the Children's Defense Fund captured the absurdity of suspension for skipping school in this pithy quote, which I used in subsequent stories about the overuse of suspension in Dayton Schools.[7] Suspension was also compounding an already-chronic problem: at least one in four middle and high school students in Dayton Public Schools missed at least six weeks of school *each year*.

There were some gems who worked in the system. I reached out to the principal at Patterson-Kennedy Elementary School, which only had one removal in the period I was investigating. "We have to develop a system that meets the needs of the kids we have, instead of trying to develop kids who meet the needs of the system," Dr. Wayne Driscoll told me.[8]

Most of our investigative work was rooted in incredulity and fueled by relationships. The stories that did require months of dedicated investigatory work, like the MCCAA story, we got because we were willing to publish things the mainstream media would not. *Dayton Daily News* reporters would later tell us that they greeted each Thursday morning with dread, worried that they would see a story in the *Voice* that they, with their much more substantial resources, had missed.

The *Dayton Voice* showed that investigative journalism can be done on a small budget. We knew how to be methodical and careful in our reporting. But our real edge? We were willing to report from the vantage of those who did not have power. And we were willing to listen to those others had written off.

LESSON LEARNED

Any work, including investigative reporting, requires a range of technical skills. But the ability to build solid, trusting relationships with those you work with is the most important one.

9

Streetwalkers and Rock Stars

With the *Dayton Voice*, "building" our business wasn't a metaphor. After nearly two years of working out of two back rooms of the American Friends Service Committee, we found some distressed but cheap office space in a turn-of-the-century building in the Santa Clara neighborhood, a business district just north of downtown Dayton. We spent the (painfully hot) summer and fall of 1995 constructing office space, building new walls, and patching and painting old ones. An ad salesperson, a former electrician, braved a 150-foot squirm through a dark, dust-laden 14-inch crawl space to lay new wiring. An editorial assistant and her husband laid the kitchen floor. More than a dozen staff and freelancers nailed, taped, and painted drywall and lugged furniture up the narrow front stairs. Jeff, co-publisher and carpenter, managed the entire project, installing everything from kitchen cabinets and counter to new computers and phones.

The move was like everything else that characterized our short history as an alternative news weekly: it was cash poor, labor heavy, slower than expected, and dependent on a lot of committed people to make it happen.

After five months of weekend construction work while continuing to publish the paper, we were ready to move into our permanent office space.[9] The curved facade of our building overlooked North Main Street on a small stretch that was an aspiring arts district. We could see Rutledge Art Gallery and the Upper Krust Sandwich shop from our windows, and we sat above Omega Records and the Color Purple Art Gallery. We had arrived in Dayton, Ohio's alternative arts community, our presence proudly displayed with a sign on the front door of 1927 N. Main.

The second-floor perch on North Main Street proved a fertile outpost for observing our small city. It was the height of the crack epidemic, and this neighborhood was like a flower trying to grow in the middle of some very cracked concrete. Looking out my office window, I started noticing a teenage girl who hung out at the entrance to the parking lot across the street. Pretty and with wavy blond hair, she looked very much like Anna, one of my foster daughters.

Her name was Casey and she was a regular, coming to the parking lot around lunchtime. Men would pull in, she would get in their cars, and they would drive away. A little while later they would drop her back off, and it would start all over again. As Sgt. Ralph Young of the Dayton Police Vice Unit later said to me, you could enroll Casey in Centerville High School (an upper middle-class suburb of Dayton) and she'd blend right in. Her resemblance to my foster daughter drew me to her, and the dissonance of her healthy appearance with street prostitution piqued my curiosity. I set out to learn more about her.

In an investigative journalism class at West Virginia University, we started the course with the students all filing up to the front of the classroom, opening a phone book to a random place, and pointing. Whatever name our finger landed on, we had to learn everything we could about that person from public records by the end of the semester. It was a good lesson in how much you could find out without ever even talking to someone, which we were not to do—just as we were to not use anything we found. Of course there was no internet, social media, or AI apps for shortcuts. This assignment required gumshoe reporting through different offices, finding property deeds, marriage and divorce records, birth records, when the person lived at what address through census records. Addresses from when a person was in high school could lead to school yearbooks that were at local libraries and had all sorts of interesting personal information. If you were really lucky, you got someone who had an arrest record.

Casey would never even make eye contact with me on the street, even though I tried to engage her. On a bad night for her, I got a break in my story. I was spending the evening on a ride-along with the Sgt. Young of the Vice Unit, learning more about prostitution hot spots in the city, when they arrested Casey. A cop who was posing as a john picked her up.

We followed. When they started driving erratically, Young flipped on his lights and siren and pulled in front of the car Casey was in. He got them both out of the car and separated them, later telling Casey that the man admitted that they had arranged sex for money.

"He's lyin'! I swear to God on my son's life he's lyin' on me. He's lyin'." She was crying. "I did not say that sir, I swear on my son's life." I had no doubt she was telling the truth; she knew something was wrong and had noticed someone tailing them so she hadn't made any deal. But she was a known prostitute with a record in a car with a cop. The details of how she handled it weren't going to carry weight. Only what the cop said was going to matter.

But now I had her full name. This led to other arrest records, which led to a string of addresses that ranged from crack houses to her step-father's house. Going to every place a public record pointed me to, over time, I strung together her tragic story of poverty, abuse, and teenage motherhood. But she never agreed to talk to me.

Another woman who was trying to get out of prostitution, Katherine, did agree to talk to me. She was in drug rehab and thought her story could be encouraging to other women trying to get out of the life. For months I tracked her struggle to stay clean and employed. One morning, at 6 a.m., our home phone rang. It was Katherine. She had been using all night and knew that if she stumbled to a bus stop in her condition she would get picked up. If she got arrested, she would have to go back to the Ohio Reformatory for Women in Marysville and complete a three-year sentence.

Jeff and I went and picked her up. She was shaking, having dry heaves, and could barely walk. She had been smoking crack, snorting heroin, and having sex with multiple men in exchange for the drugs. "I just need time—I'll be okay," she assured us. We put her on the futon in our home office where she could recover in privacy.

Eventually Katherine told me more than she had told anyone, about multiple assaults and eventually about being sexually abused by her step-father when she was a teenager. Her mother was still married to him, and he still came to Katherine offering money for sex. If she was using, she took the money and did what she was paid for. After eight months of re-porting, I published my final stories on prostitution, which also featured women who had successfully left the life. In the story about Katherine, I referred to her stepfather, who still came to her for sex, as "her last john." While she wasn't named in the story, she was furious at me for that.[10]

Weeks after the prostitution stories ran in 1997, the *Voice* staff gathered with a full-house crowd at Celebrity Nightclub for the paper's first-ever local lifetime achievement awards in music.[11] Dayton was thick with musicians. Most of the people associated with the *Voice*, from editorial staff to advertising and distribution staff, were in or associated with a band. Sometimes it seemed like there were as many musicians in Dayton as there were autoworkers a couple decades before.

Don Thrasher was the *Voice's* music writer. A drummer, he played with Guided by Voices, Swearing at Motorists, and a range of other bands. He was an informed and elegant writer, and he elevated the *Voice's* stature with his credibility. Nick Kizirnis, an amazing surf guitarist, became our art director in 1996, rescuing us from some very bad early design. They and other *Voice* staff helped shape our music events, which we held regularly. The March 1997 event was our first annual music awards. Our plan was to launch the Dayton Music Hall of Fame after five years of these awards. In the interim, the Hall of Fame was literally a hallway in the *Voice* where framed photos of the awardees were hung.

The large club was packed. We were honoring the Dayton-based funk band the Ohio Players, bluegrass musician Red Allen, and jazz musician Lester Bass. The honorees drew a crowd that represented Dayton's population, which was roughly half African American and half Appalachian. While their hits "Fire" and "Love Rollercoaster" played, Sugarfoot Bonner and Diamond Williams accepted the award for the Ohio Players, dressed as flamboyantly as they did in the 1970s. Then bluegrass rang out ("I Just Came to Get My Baby out of Jail") as Greg Allen accepted the award for his late father, Red, a pioneer of contemporary bluegrass music.

Finally, refined and soft-spoken jazz bassist and trombonist Lester Bass, who played with Lionel Hampton and Dizzy Gillespie, took the stage. "It's an honor that my Dayton friends and family think that much of me," he said. "Thank you so much. I love you all."

It was a heady night—for the musicians, for their families, for the unique mix of people who were rarely in the same room. They may not have listened to each other's music much, but they understood its cultural power and the sacrifice required to spend a lifetime committed to making it.

Our special events always boosted morale. They centered the cultural role the paper played in the city, and they brought our readers together as the eclectic community that they were. But they didn't slow down the relentless demand of the weekly publication schedule. The day after the awards, Jeff was no doubt fixing something in the office while I cleaned the bathrooms, and then it was back to work on Monday to hit the Tuesday night printing schedule.

LESSON LEARNED

Honor the talents of your staff team. Every ability that they bring, no matter how seemingly unrelated to the primary work, can help you achieve your mission while building a solid and unique work culture.

10

You Are Free to Go

Part of a gaggle of reporters, several wielding large TV cameras, I watched as Jenny Wilcox stood at a counter at the Montgomery County Courthouse waiting for a clerk to give her a bag of meager personal effects. When the man behind the counter said he couldn't find them, it was one last overwhelming detail. Jenny broke down and started sobbing.

Eleven years she had been in prison. Eleven years. Jenny Wilcox and her friend Dale Aldridge were casualties of a child sex abuse hysteria that swept the country in the 1980s and early 1990s. The McMartin preschool case in California, which became the longest and most expensive criminal trial in US history, was the most famous of these. Jenny and Dale's case, like so many others, was characterized by no solid evidence, shifting testimony, and manipulated child witnesses.

When Jenny was ultimately released on March 8, 1996, I had been covering this story for more than two years. I had maintained regular contact with Jenny throughout that time. I couldn't just stand there and watch her sob with all of these cameras pointed at her. I left the group of reporters and approached her.[12]

I introduced myself. "Jenny, it's Marrianne." While we had spent days in the same courtroom, we had never really met. She crumpled into my arms and cried harder. Eventually, they found her belongings and we walked down the corridor and out of the courthouse, trailed by reporters with their cameras. She was free.

We had only been publishing our scrappy little weekly a few months when private investigator Marty Yant showed up with a story pitch and a foot-high pile of documents about the 1984 Wilcox-Aldridge case. At the time, in addition to starting this small business, I was a foster mother to Katie Martin, 13, the fifth of the six Martin girls. And I was in graduate school. I remember how that lofty stack of depositions, arrest reports, and court transcripts about the case haunted me, sitting there in the corner on top of my filing cabinet, waiting for me.

Marty was a credible private investigator. He had several major stories under his belt, including the investigation of the Montgomery County Community Action Agency that we had already published. His thoroughness was evident when I did finally plow through those papers, growing increasingly horrified at the obvious railroading of two innocent people and the gross manipulation and intimidation of child witnesses.

I started working with Marty on crafting the first story, which led our first anniversary edition in August 1994. "Three of the six who testified against a couple for sexual abuse 10 years ago now say: 'It Didn't Happen.' But two people remain in prison. For life."[13] The kicker, headline, and subhead told the story. The "it didn't happen" part of the headline was in 72-point type. The three boys, now men, who recanted their testimony were three of the six juveniles who originally testified against Jenny and Dale.

Marty's account went back to the original trial in 1985 and detailed the inconsistencies in the evidence. One girl's statement, which fluctuated in details about who was involved and what was done, told of a level of abuse that would have left physical evidence. A medical exam showed no evidence to support her testimony. One boy—the oldest of three brothers who were the first ones to recant—was held in juvenile detention until he "told the truth." Eventually he and his brothers told stories of molestation that they thought the adults around them wanted to hear. But then the details didn't match. Another child testified that Jenny, who has cerebral palsy and had no use of her left arm, grabbed three boys and pulled them into her apartment by herself. Other stories were a strange amalgam of childhood fears with sexual overtones, such as a girl who said she was shot with an injection in her vagina. Many stories involved photography, but no evidence of film, negatives, or Polaroids was found.

At Glenburn Green apartments, the low-income housing complex where Jenny lived, sex abuse hysteria was rampant. On at least one occasion, a group of men with knives surrounded a single man, accusing him of sex abuse and threatening to castrate him. The targets for the accusations were as random as the stories. Adults spun increasingly hysterical tales, and their children, as children do, chimed in with loyalty and enthusiasm. The lies were horrific and spectacular, without any evidence to support them.

Here's what was true: Jenny had had an affair with the husband of one of the most vociferously accusatory mothers. And Jenny had let numerous young people, like Aldridge, stay in her apartment, creating a noise level that was frequently annoying to her neighbors. It came out in subsequent, postconviction proceedings that 22 children and 20 adults at Glenburn Green apartments were named as suspects at one time or another for sexually molesting children. But it is likely that these details that made Jenny and Dale unpopular were the real reasons the people who lived in the housing complex chose them to name as perpetrators.

Marty's first story in the *Voice* on this case detailed the 1985 trial, which ended with guilty verdicts and life sentences for Jenny and Dale. "As the bailiff read their guilty verdicts on all counts, Wilcox, a 24-year-old mother of two, turned white, trembled and pulled her hair back on her head. Then she began screaming. As deputies rushed her out of the courtroom, the stunned 20-year-old Aldridge remained silently behind."

A week after our August 1994 story, the Montgomery County prosecutor's office responded to a petition to vacate Jenny and Dale's sentences. They argued that since the three young men who had recanted testified under oath during the original trial, their testimony as children was more valid than their testimony as adults. That alone was the prosecutorial argument.

The judge granted Jenny an evidentiary hearing. Delays and continuances ensued over the next year, and we continued to follow every development in the case. During this time Jenny's original attorney was suspended from practice by the Dayton Bar Association, in part for lax defense of clients. (He hadn't called a single witness in support of either defendant during their initial trial.)

Finally, three years after half the witnesses recanted their testimony, Jenny and Dale got a real hearing, with a well-researched and fair case argued on their behalf, complete with medical and psychological testing, and expert and eyewitnesses.[14]

As the three recanting witnesses took the stand, Prosecutor Linda Howland aggressively and suggestively Mirandized them. "Whatever you say can be held against you. Do you understand that?" And: "You can stop answering questions at any time. Do you understand that?" I watched as the first brother sunk further into the seat as each question was asked, clearly reacting to the intimidation tactics as intended. But he and his brothers all held up and told a simple, consistent story of how they were bullied into telling stories of abuse that never happened.

When a physician for one of the girls who had testified at the trial was called to the stand, the prosecutor implied that the doctor could be sued for his testimony. "Now you quit it," the judge barked, pointing at the prosecutor. "You're not going to sit there and tell the witness that he'll be sued. I'm not going to have it." While the judge had allowed bullying of the former child witnesses, he didn't tolerate the tactic when applied to an expert witness.

The doctor said that the mother of an eight-year-old girl reported her daughter had been sexually molested by four males and one female, all over the age of 18. Allegedly, both rectal and vaginal penetration had occurred four to five times. The doctor found no bruising or torn or traumatized tissue. "I would have expected some positive findings, which I did not find."

In response, all the prosecution could do was suggest that the perpetrators might have had very small penises and used a lot of lubrication.

Then came the defense's expert testimony about witness coercion and the suggestibility of children, about "mass psychogenic illness" and how it can take place in a community like an apartment complex. Richard J. Ofshe, PhD, of the University of California, Berkeley, who coauthored *Making Monsters: False Memories, Psychotherapy, and Sexual Hysteria*,[15] testified that he had never seen a case of child witness intimidation that was this extreme. "I haven't seen these tactics used in this way with this degree of demonstration of power brought to bear on children. This is unique in my experience."

Another witness, Melvin Guyer, PhD, a professor of forensic law in the Department of Psychiatry at the University of Michigan, talked about the changing stories of the accusers. "There's something static about the truth and something permeable about contrivances." Others testified about the hysteria at the apartment complex at the time, with one man describing how he was surrounded by men with knives who threatened to castrate him. Expert witnesses put that hysteria into a broader, social context, explaining how those dynamics start, spread, and escalate. Still another testified to Jenny's gentle character and willingness to watch other people's children.

It was a full, complete, and competent hearing. Three weeks later, Judge Richard Parrott overturned the convictions. Twenty-four years later, 35 years after the first false accusations, the state of Ohio settled a wrongful conviction case with Jenny and Dale.

Early in our coverage of the Wilcox-Aldridge story, the fifth of the six Martin girls, Katie, was living with us. Bright and spirited, Katie was in the seventh grade when she moved in. The first two girls who lived with us, Norah and Anna, had found way too much trouble on the streets of Dayton to safely stay with us. Norah ran away, lived on the streets for a short period, and then ended up getting arrested and spending the rest of her teenage years in a juvenile correctional facility. Anna returned to a rural children's home, where she finished high school. We had higher hopes for Katie, who was younger and clearly found comfort in being part of a family.

We also had learned from our early fostering experience. We were not going to allow for unprogrammed and unsupervised time, even though a child raised in normal circumstances would be fine at home on their own at the age of 13. We enrolled Katie in an after-school program where she would have activities with her peers, in addition to group and individual therapy. Every hour we were working, she had supervision.

From the time Katie was six, when I first met her, she would compulsively take things. Change, cookies, trinkets. Her pockets would always be full of something. It would be years before I became familiar with the myriad consequences of trauma, and still years before "trauma-informed treatment" became common in the therapeutic world. Would it have made a difference with my girls if the clinical approach to their behaviors started with "what happened to you?" instead of "what's wrong with you?" I think so.

But I understood little, and services offered to foster kids were minimal. Foster parents got $10 a day to feed kids, and an occasional clothing allowance. That's pretty much it. It's like the whole system believed that what doesn't kill you makes you stronger. It turns out, though, that what doesn't kill you, like your parents abandoning you, can really fuck you up.

When Jenny and I left the courthouse on that March day when she was freed, we came to an intersection on our way to get something to eat. Jenny looked up at the signal. "What does that mean?" she asked. It took me a moment to realize that she was looking at the lit-up, white symbol of the walking person. "It means it's okay to walk," I told her.

It was Jenny's first free walk after nearly 12 years, and international symbols were just the first of many changes she was to notice. Those first 10 minutes of freedom, as the two of us walked from the courthouse to a restaurant, felt unreal to both of us. With all of the challenges now facing Jenny—where to live, reestablishing her relationship with her two children, now 12 and 15, how to make a living—she could only think of the simplest things. "I don't even know what my favorite color is anymore," she said as we sat down to lunch. The very idea of making any decisions, such as picking what she wanted to eat, was exhilarating but overwhelming.

A little more than a year later, as we were preparing the fourth anniversary issue of the *Voice*, Jenny stopped by the office as she passed through town on her way to visit friends. It had been 18 months since the hearing, but the prosecutor's office was still considering recharging the case. Jenny was struggling but adapting. It wasn't until December of that year when the charges were dropped.

My formative years were good ones for journalism. I was going into seventh grade when Bob Woodward and Carl Bernstein broke the Watergate story in the summer of 1972, which eventually ended the presidency of Richard M. Nixon. Three years before, Seymour Hersh had broken the

My Lai Massacre story, which exposed not just the crimes of "Charlie Company," one army infantry battalion, but the crimes of the entire Vietnam War. In high school I dug into these and other stories. I was trying to understand my country, but I ended up enthralled with the potential of journalism to provide a check on power.

The way I covered the Wilcox-Aldridge story is not exactly how I was trained in journalism at West Virginia University. The journalistic "remove" that was encouraged would never have me taking a subject of the news into my arms while she cried. Nor would it have us so aggressively taking sides in a story. But the "new journalism" that incorporated personal narrative in stories and advocacy journalism that aggressively took a stand were ascending and influential as I started practicing journalism in the late 1970s. More recently, scholars Lawrence R. Frey and Kevin M. Carragee explored "communication activism" in a three-volume set of case studies.[16] In one chapter John P. McHale, from Illinois State University, discussed his experience of working on the documentary *Unreasonable Doubt: The Joe Amrine Case* (2002), which focused on a wrongly convicted man in Missouri.[17] The publicity brought by the documentary eventually led to the exoneration of Joe Amrine, even though he had been on death row and exhausted the appeals process.

We took sides at the *Dayton Voice*—but only after thoroughly investigating the story. In many stories that we covered, there came a point when the truth was obvious. So obvious, in fact, that it would be irresponsible to go on covering it in a "balanced" way that essentially requires you to quote people you know are lying. Truth was the goal, not objectivity.

Not everyone we sided with was as thoroughly vindicated as Jenny and Dale. And powerful people who found themselves in our stories often attacked our credibility. Some even threatened to sue. But none of the attacks survived our follow-up, and no one ever sued. We never regretted a side that we took.

In journalism ethics classes, this is a standard challenge: You are at the scene of a horrific accident or natural disaster. Someone is lying there bleeding. Do you take pictures of them and ask them how it feels, or do you take action to staunch the wound? Like many ethical questions, the first answer is typically "it depends." It depends on whether there are medical personnel there to provide care. It depends on whether the journalist is put in danger by attending to the victim or staying on the scene. It depends on consideration of legal liability. (Really, someone always goes there.)

I was consistently alarmed at how absolute my fellow journalism students, and later fellow journalists, were about staying out of the story, even if it meant quietly witnessing a horror that they could do something about. I would always staunch the wound. Every time.

I was a fan of Jack Newfield, an investigative reporter who did much of his influential work with the *Village Voice*. I loved his participatory, emotionally engaged reporting. When he covered the 1968 Democratic National Convention in Chicago, he threw a typewriter from the window of his hotel at police who were beating demonstrators. Anger, he said, "improves lucidity, persistence, audacity, and memory." You can feel that anger in a 1972 *Village Voice* essay that he wrote about "new journalism." In that piece, he provides us with an eloquent description of objectivity.

"Objectivity can be defined as the way the mass media reported the history of the Vietnam War before the Pentagon Papers; the way the racism in the North was covered before Watts; the way auto safety was reported before Ralph Nader," Newfield wrote.

> Objectivity is the media printing Nelson Rockefeller's lies about Attica
> until the facts came out that the state troopers and not the inmates had
> killed all the hostages; that the troopers used outlawed dum dum bul
> lets; that 350 inmates including some badly wounded, were beaten after
> they gave up. Objectivity is printing a dozen stories about minor welfare
> frauds, but not a word about the My Lai massacre until Seymour Hersh.
> Objectivity is not covering the stomping of the gay activists at the Inner
> Circle dinner because Micky Maye's union paid for a table. Objectivity
> is ignoring George McGovern as a joke after he won the Wisconsin pri
> mary. Objectivity is believing people with power and printing their press
> releases. Objectivity is not shouting "liar" in a crowded country.[18]

The Dayton Voice shouted "liar" over the wrongful convictions of Jenny Wilcox and Dale Aldridge. Not many truths are powerful enough to save lives. But this one was.

LESSON LEARNED

Lies can gather incredible momentum. If you know the truth, speak it. Look for allies, yes, but engage the fight.

11

Heartbreaks on the Labor Beat

As each metal part went through the plating process at Hohman Plating and Manufacturing in Dayton, Ohio, workers went with it. Throughout this nonautomated assembly line, men pushed and pulled automotive and other parts in and out of tanks of acids to clean them, and tanks of liquid chrome, nickel, copper, and other metals to coat them. Thousands of parts, some as small as bolts and others as big as bumpers, were pulled through the process every day. When the liquid metals needed to be kept cold, the men worked in the cold; when the metal baths needed to kept hot, the men worked in the heat. Every day, all day, they were exposed to toxic chemicals that burned, poisoned, and scarred them.

In late November 1996, about a third of the 91 employees at Hohman Plating went on strike over safety conditions at the plant.[19] November is a lousy time of year to go on strike. Working where they did, though, these clearly weren't people who made decisions based on personal comfort. In a gritty industrial corridor just off I-75 on Dayton's north side, they walked the picket line daily as winter set in. They had a small trailer parked there, where picketers could get coffee, water, and warmth and where supporters could drop off food. In that small trailer, at a collapsible Formica table, they told me their stories of 115-degree–Fahrenheit work areas and catwalks with no protective railings over acid tanks. And burns—lots of burns. Every interview I conducted there was punctuated with a rolled-up pantleg or shirt sleeve or a lifted T-shirt to show a scar from an injury at the plant. Every one.[20]

The brutality of many workplaces is hidden. The journalistic tradition of exposing those dark corners is long. In 1906 Upton Sinclair published *The Jungle*,[21] a novel that portrayed the harsh working conditions of immigrants in the meatpacking industry. Sinclair was also a journalist, and he gathered information for *The Jungle* by working undercover in the Chicago stockyards.

In 1974 Studs Terkel took a different but no less radical approach with his book *Working: People Talk about What They Do All Day and How They Feel about What They Do.*[22] An oral historian, Terkel was committed to capturing the first-person accounts of life that rarely make it into daily newspapers, let alone the annals of history. In my graduate studies, I was learning more about the importance of messengers in persuasion. I was increasingly asking myself who the most authentic and authoritative messengers were for any story. With my dog-eared copy of *Working* as a guide, I decided the workers at the plant would be the only sources for the story about Hohman.

In a *Dayton Voice* story on December 18, 1996,[23] we featured the first-person accounts of 10 men, ages 20 to 42, who worked at the plant and were participating in the strike. Kevin Vance, 23, described pumping chemicals out of 55-gallon drums by hand, explaining that the scars on his face resulted from getting splashed when he removed the pump from a drum of nitric acid. Greg Harshman, 38, told of falling into a tank of sulfuric acid from a flimsy "tank board," which was just a piece of plywood. The force he used to move a stuck piece of pipe caused him to fall off the tank board. He landed up to his waist in a 40 percent sulfuric acid mixture. A co-worker had told him that if he ever fell into an acid tank he should jump into the rinse tank, which he did. He was so new he didn't even know where the showers were or which chemicals he could safely rinse off with water.

Many stories reflected the risk of specific chemicals. Acid and cyanide together, for example, make cyanide gas. Cyanide is used in the plating process because it prevents some metals from crystalizing, keeping them in a liquid state. There were often bags of cyanide piled on the floor, and acid spills happened. If acid and cyanide mixed, the plant could become a giant gas chamber. The most graphic stories they told were of chrome sores—when workers used razor blades to cut the chrome out of their flesh. "It's like a festered splinter that keeps boring in there if you don't cut it out," said Jeff Disney, 32, about when chrome gets into your bloodstream. "I had it so bad one time, I had a red line coming up from my thumb and past my wrist from an infection from the chrome."

Going to doctors and hospitals was discouraged by management. You tended to your own wounds and kept going. If men did leave to go to the hospital, they drove themselves.

Compared to Hohman Plating, which few people would ever enter, hospitals are much more visible workplaces. But the same motivation—making the most money possible—drove dangerous outcomes in both settings.

In January 1997 nurses at Franciscan Medical Center in Dayton started organizing a union. Their first meeting drew a handful of people, their second 60. They announced their third meeting citywide, and 200 people attended. At that point, Dayton became the only city in the country where there was a drive to organize nurses in every hospital in the city.

Of all the area's hospitals, Franciscan had seen the most dramatic decline in nursing staff—a 28.6 percent drop from 1990 to 1997.[24] During this time, according to the hospital's reports to the IRS, inpatient services remained steady while outpatient services increased. And those who were inpatients were sicker than previous patients had been. They had "higher acuity rates," meaning they had more severe conditions and needed a higher degree of care, which there were fewer nurses to provide.

"It's gotten to the point," said one woman who had been a nurse for 16 years, "that when we know someone who is going into the hospital, we tell them, 'you better bring along a friend or family member so that someone can take care of you.'"

One nurse, Vicki Moots, explained the implications for staffing. "Fifteen, 20 years ago we would have 18 patients on a ward. Six would just be getting tests, one third would have just had surgery and had IVs, tubes and dressing changes. They'd need to be coaxed out of bed for the first time. They took lots of care. And another third would be well on their way to recovery. They'd have no tubes or IVs and would be up and about basically taking care of themselves."

"The first and third group are no longer in the hospital," Moots continued. "They are still in the acute phase when they go home. Now all 18 would be very acute—with the same staffing."

These changes were driven by business considerations and had bottom-line results. Given that these hospitals are classified as nonprofits,

the publicly filed information on their finances is abundant. It's the price
they pay for not paying taxes. We poured through Dayton hospitals' IRS
990s to cull as much financial information as we could for Dayton hospitals during this period when practices were changing so dramatically.

At Franciscan Hospital we found that the hospital's revenues increased by 10.4 percent between 1993 and 1995. During that same time,
pay and benefits for program and service staff, which includes nurses,
went up by just 2.1 percent. Physician fees, though, went up by 33 percent.
And management and general salaries, in this three-year period, went up
by *66 percent*.[25]

All the additional cash Franciscan had? The nurses said that some of
it should be spent on direct care for the patients through higher levels of
nurse staffing. In subsequent years correlations between nursing staffing
and patient outcomes, including infection and mortality rates, became
so clear that they drove legislation requiring at least the public posting of
staffing rates in hospitals. But nurses didn't need those studies to understand the impact of reduced staffing levels.

The nurses' organizing drive was spurred by what always motivates
union organizing: management greed that subverts the goals of the organization and exploits the people they most need to fulfill those goals.
Unions are a check on power in the workplace just like the media is a
check on corporations and public bodies. Without greed, perhaps the
check would not be needed. But there's always greed. There's always a lot
of greed.

In February 1997, OSHA fined Hohman Plating and Manufacturing
$200,000 for 87 safety violations. In the same week that the fines were
announced, the company signed a contract with the union, and the striking workers returned to the job.[26]

In July of that same year, the nurses at Franciscan Medical Center
held a union recognition vote. The vote count took place on a Friday night.
At 10:45 p.m. Jeff and I were in the parking lot of the building where the
vote was counted when we saw one of the organizing nurses in tears running to her car, while another was walking quickly to hers. Others rushed
after them to comfort them. Few weren't crying.

The Registered Nurse bargaining unit, which would have represented the first organized health care workers in Dayton, was defeated by 45 votes; 276 RNs voted for the union, 321 voted against.[27] While the nurses had been confident of victory two months before the election, the battle against the union intensified dramatically in the final weeks. The hospital employed a consultant, Management Science Associates, to help wage a campaign against the union. Hospital management routinely took staff aside during work hours for meetings during which union participation would be discouraged. In the month before the election, the National Labor Relations Board issued a formal complaint against the hospital for reprimanding employees who were distributing union literature. The hospital also emphasized the danger of strikes, even though hospital strikes are rare and contract provisions require the support of a vast majority, typically more than 80 percent, of staff.

Management's most effective strategy, though, was implemented just a week before the election: a letter from Franciscan CEO James Strieby apologizing for all of the staff cuts and promising to improve staffing levels. The timing of this tactic made it clear that management thought the union election would be successful. They weren't going to make this admission and promise unless it was absolutely necessary. Since staffing levels were the main impetus behind the union drive, the letter proved very persuasive, nurses said, and led many employees to conclude that a union was not necessary.

Labor was a heartbreaking beat. Working people would risk everything to stand up for themselves and fix their workplaces. All too frequently, the gains they won would be minimal or they would be crushed by the overwhelming power of their employers, which have labor laws predominantly on their side.

Labor used to be a regular beat at many newspapers. Fifty years ago, a third of US workers belonged to unions; now it's 1 in 10. As organized labor shrank, labor beats disappeared and were replaced by "workplace" reporters in business sections, whose sources were most frequently business owners.

No matter what the fate of organized labor, though, where there is greed and too few checks on power there will be stories. Upton Sinclair's *The Jungle* was widely credited for leading to the passage of the Federal Meat Inspection Act of 1906,[28] which set higher sanitary standards in meatpacking plants that led to greater safety for workers. When Sinclair wrote about workers losing fingers while working with the dangerous machinery they used to cut and process meat, people were far more horrified by the idea that those fingers were in their family meatloaf than they were by the permanent maiming of workers. But that they were horrified at all was the result of dogged journalism.

If media attention is the sunshine that acts as a disinfectant, it's needed most in these dark corners of our economy.

LESSON LEARNED

Access to communication channels is a privilege. If you have that access, look for those who don't and tell their stories with them.

12

Bad Art and Crisis Management

Early every Thursday morning throughout the 1990s, the corner of North Main Street and Santa Clara Avenue was piled high with stacks of bundled copies of the *Dayton Voice*. The pile grew smaller as one of the most interesting workforces imaginable showed up and filled their trunks, back seats, and truck beds with issues of the paper. Many of them were freelance writers for the *Voice* and local artists and musicians, cobbling together multiple modest income streams. Within a couple hours, the *Voice* would be in boxes and newsstands throughout Montgomery and Greene Counties.

On April 2, 1997, though, we hadn't even made all the deliveries before we started receiving calls about the issue. "How could the *Voice* print such a racist image on its cover?" incredulous *Voice* readers asked. The cover story was about domestic violence, tracking the stories of two women—one Black and one white—who had been killed by their partners. The cover illustration was an attempt to depict a man in the shadows with his victim in the foreground but instead looked like a Black man menacing a white woman.[29]

"Picking up a copy of the *Dayton Voice*, a feeling of disbelief, hurt and outrage filled me," one letter writer said in the next edition. "A depiction of a black man with animalistic features was shown attacking a white woman with bruises on her face."[30]

The night before, as we prepared the paper for publication, we saw that the image could be interpreted that way. Jeff and I worked with the art director on the image, tweaking the contrast and other details. The visible features of the man's face were decidedly European, we told ourselves, and his more prominent forearm and hand were the same color as the victim. We convinced ourselves it was okay. It was time to put the paper to bed, and we didn't see an alternative approach to the art.

The mistake was evident immediately. The face in the image printed darker than it looked on the final galleys. People sent us images from white supremacist publications that were eerily similar. As they came into the office, we gathered the staff together around our meeting table in the center of the office to decide what to do. We were collectively mortified, horrified even. Shame is not something I've had much experience with, but I knew that dark feeling that morning.

The paper couldn't stay out there that way, we decided. We called our printer, the *Troy Daily News*, and explained what happened and said we needed to reprint the cover, dropping the image of the man out entirely and adding an explanation that this was a reprinted cover. The printer was amazingly responsive and accommodating, postponing their planned print jobs to immediately run a new cover.

We called back our distribution staff and started a phone tree to mobilize volunteers to help us gather up papers, bring them back to the *Voice* office, and rewrap each issue with the new cover. We replaced 12,000 of the 22,000 covers on the stand. It was a massive undertaking, and dozens of people spent the next two days rewrapping the paper and then delivering it all over again.

Media critique was our origin story. If we didn't think the mainstream media was failing our community so badly, we wouldn't have started our own newspaper. Now we had our own flamboyant media failure.

After the initial flurry of cover-replacing activity, we knew we must cover the mistake as a story. A formal apology had to come from us, but we needed someone not on our staff or in our regular freelance pool to report on the incident. I reached out to a journalism professor at the University of Dayton, Debbie Juniewicz, who agreed to do the story.

She interviewed at least a dozen sources, including civil rights leaders and a local professor, who used the two covers to start a discussion among students. One of my former graduate school professors, Danny Robinson, gamely put forth what is called the "psychological interpretation theory" of communication, explaining that people make meaning of what they see based on their own historic exposure to images. They can fill in blanks that aren't necessarily in the specific image they are looking at.[31]

The history, though, is real, as are the images and the dangerous messages they convey. It's a history that we collectively share and know. "In a society that has done so little to overcome its racist past and present, such an image is another assault on black men who are too frequently the real victims in our society," we wrote in our apology on the cover of the next week's issue. "Whatever our intention, to publish an illustration that could be so misinterpreted was an unconscionable error."

Replacing the cover also caused its own set of reactions, from people saying we were trying to cover up our mistake to others saying we were going overboard to be politically correct. We addressed that in our apology. "We want to make it clear that the decision to reprint was a decision to take a toxic image off the streets, not to cover up our mistake. That error is a matter of the permanent record. We hope our decision to correct our own mistake may in some way contribute to a further dialogue about racism."[32]

The crisis management lessons here are not new. Own your mistake quickly and publicly. Participate in an open dialogue about it, and invite critics to voice their perspectives. In crisis communication, the goal is to get the controversy off the public stage. Because we followed good crisis communication practices—in this case out of sheer earnestness rather than strategy—the discussion of the cover was soon over and it had little impact on us as an organization. If anything, our response became a positive part of our brand.

Personally, I had more to reconcile. Looking back on it now, it's striking to me that I didn't feel blamed by the other staff. I was the editor, I knew that it could be a problem, and I put the paper to bed anyway. Jeff, the last person working with the art director before taking the galleys to Troy, said he felt most responsible.

But this was consistent with how I have made most of my mistakes at work. My strengths are in execution. In Myers-Briggs terminology, I'm a strong "J," or judger—I bring things to conclusion rather than gather more information like a "P," or perceiver, would. In the Clifton Strengths measurement I am high on discipline, responsibility, accountability—all characteristics related to being able to execute a plan and land the deliverable. The flip side of this, though, is that I can be too ready to call something done when it is not. To fail to give something one more close look before doing the final save. To be overly reluctant to change a plan when a change is clearly called for.

It's not enough to know your strengths and weaknesses in a workplace. You have to communicate them, particularly your weaknesses and particularly if you are the boss. Give your colleagues and your staff the information they need to understand when you are most likely to make a mistake and give them permission to intercede. My weak point, always, is wanting to be finished. At a recent retreat with my current staff at Chapin Hall at the University of Chicago, my current workplace, we were coming up with one-word descriptions of each other. One of my staff's one word for me: *Now*.

So I need to say to my team: Challenge me when I'm overly reluctant to change a plan or timeline. Push me to move deadlines out further when that is an option. Review web content I've written one more time before I press post. Proofread important messages before I send. If something doesn't feel good or right, honor that feeling and respond accordingly. Slow me the fuck down. Please.

LESSON LEARNED

A good leader knows their weaknesses and lets others know them, too. With enough trust in your team, your colleagues will be able to protect you from the risks those weaknesses create.

13

Too Much Skin in the Game

Our dog Idgie Threadgood would lie in the front entry room of the *Dayton Voice* and greet visitors. She was typically the only one in that room. The UPS guy was a regular, delivering promotional items that we would all share—CDs, movies, books for us to review. "UPS," he'd yell as he entered. "Federal Express," we would all yell back. One day he got wise to us and yelled "Federal Express" so we would all have to yell "UPS."

The *Voice* was the most fun most of us could ever imagine having at work. It was also the most misery. Long days, no vacation—hell, barely any weekends—and an increasingly unfeasible business model. We started the *Voice* after the alternative weekly heydays of the late '80s and early '90s. Classifieds, particularly personals, were a major financial driver. By the end of the '90s, those revenue streams were disappearing, going online. Even without that development, though, the poverty of Dayton combined with its small size was unlikely to ever provide a market for enough advertising to support a free circulation weekly.

A lot of people invested in the paper to keep it going, and we went into considerable personal debt. We would issue paychecks on Friday and ask people not to cash them until Monday while a few more advertising checks cleared. We paid ourselves less than we paid our staff, which wasn't much.

Our son, Brendan Isaac Epton, was born in December of 1998. At the same time, the sixth and youngest of the Martin girls was finishing high school. Leaving Dayton now, I would not feel like I was another adult abandoning them. And our little neighborhood of Five Oaks was breaking down. The crack epidemic and the omnipresence of guns were taking their toll. In the preceding year, two children had been killed by gunfire within blocks of our house. And I knew the sorry state of public schools firsthand through my foster children. Dayton was becoming an increasingly difficult place to make a living and to raise a child.

A year later, I wrote a goodbye column in the *Voice* as we prepared to move to Chicago.[33] In it, I addressed the persistent financial precariousness of our operation and the personal stress that caused, but I also explained why we had kept going. "What we will be most proud of is that we started an institution, a for-profit business that is unique for one reason more than any other: it was, and is, designed to do good. It was designed to honor the heroes in our community and to expose those who abuse power, to be pro-woman and anti-racist, and to celebrate the culture and spirit of this community."

It was also possible to move on with confidence because of the team that was in place, particularly Editor Kristen Wicker and Advertising Director Daniel Emerich. In the edgy rock band that was our staff, they were the band leaders.

We had spent seven years on this roller coaster that could have us tending to a recovering junkie on our futon one week and celebrating with Grammy-winning musicians the next. We had a bit too much skin in this game, and, more than once, it left us bleeding on the floor. After we left, it took us more than a dozen years to slowly climb out of debt. But the lessons learned have lasted my entire career.

As I moved on to other roles and to supervise larger groups of people, I increasingly became a student of management and was endlessly interested in the question of what makes people happiest and most productive at work. Over time, management books and the *Harvard Business Review* got redundant. The main lessons are simple. People want to excel at what they are good at, and they want to apply those efforts to something meaningful. They want transparency—no management secrets—and they don't want stupid rules and needless bureaucracy. And they want to be themselves at work. If they get all of that, the recognition and sense of belonging that is so important to all of us follow. Our jobs become something important to us—a place not only where we want to be but also where we thrive and become our best selves.

More than any other place I've worked at or managed, the *Dayton Voice* fulfilled these best-in-class management principles. It was a place where a unique collection of people figured out, week after week, how to keep rowing in the same direction. Everyone felt like it was their boat—because it was. And even though we never got to our desired destination—a secure business with a positive balance sheet—the stops we made along the way were nothing short of glorious.

LESSON LEARNED

There is a line between commitment to a mission and making a sacrifice that compromises your and your family's well-being. Be attentive to that line, and be ready to make a change.

Part Three

The Labor Movement

14

What Democracy Looks Like

It was early 2000, and I was at my first all-staff meeting at my new job with Illinois Council 31 of the American Federation of State, County and Municipal Employees (AFSCME). New century, new job, new city (Chicago). After covering labor as a reporter for years, I was excited to be on the other side—working as the public affairs director for a labor union to get the stories of working people in the media and in front of elected officials.

More than 100 AFSCME staff filled round tables in a large hotel conference room in Springfield, Illinois. I eventually learned that this action-oriented staff hated these staff meetings and did everything they could to keep them as short as possible. Being the newbie, though, I found everything interesting. As various staff raised their hands and shared information or asked a question, I watched as they received a handwritten note after they finished speaking. Each one of them looked at it and then smiled or laughed. Then I got up and said something, but nobody handed me the note.

I asked my new work friend Linc Cohen what was in the note that others had been handed. He got it and shared it with me. It said: "Shut the fuck up." A blunt, witty rebuke to those who were making the meeting longer. I thought it was hysterical.

Of all the workplaces I have ever been in, AFSCME was the funniest. It was also a place I felt at home. It became clear that management— the president and secretary treasurer of the union—hired people from similar backgrounds, with similar achievements. Most of us grew up in working-class families but went on to finish college and, frequently, graduate school. I remember how direct the questions were in the interview process about my perceptions of working people and who is most likely

to be in the vanguard of the labor movement. They didn't want employees
with romantic notions of the working class. I didn't have any of those.

We had sold our three-bedroom, frame house in Dayton for the princely
sum of $49,000. At the time I thought any job that paid $35K would be
fantastic, so that's what I asked for. I had no idea what other people made
and what I could potentially make. I was just about to turn 40 and had
never made a decent salary, never had or put a penny into a retirement account. But I was just beginning to learn that the experience and education
I had acquired over the last decade qualified me for higher-paying jobs.
Within a few months of starting, AFSCME gave me a substantial raise.
When it was clear that I could deliver, they couldn't, in good conscience,
pay me less than other staff just because I was naive.

    AFSCME was my introduction to directly and effectively communi-
cating with policymakers, in this case state legislators. The three-person
legislative staff—Bill Perkins, Ray Harris, and Kurt Anderson—knew every marble corner of the Illinois statehouse and what messages would
(and wouldn't) reach its denizens.

    While AFSCME represented a largely secure and well-paid part of
the workforce—public employees—it was starting to organize a growing
low-wage workforce: home health care providers. When organizing new
members, unions like to demonstrate just what a union can do for them.
So while our organizing shop was out talking to and organizing workers,
our legislative team was working on winning a one-dollar-an-hour raise for
home health care workers who were paid by the state. We identified state
senators and representatives who would sponsor and support the initiative, and we developed a detailed database of home health care workers by
legislative district. When efforts to get media coverage for the campaign
led to minimal results, we switched to a letter-to-the-editor campaign.
I wrote about 10 model letters with key messages and circulated them
to AFSCME field staff, who in turn worked with dozens of home health
care workers to customize their letters and send them to local newspapers. The legislative staff set up lobbying visits between workers and their
state representatives. Soon, the dollar-an-hour campaign was common

knowledge, with no significant opposition. The eventual legislative win boosted AFSCME's organizing campaign throughout the state.

At AFSCME I also learned what a good electoral ground game looks like. All staff worked from polls open to polls close every election day. We targeted districts, mobilized and supervised our members who did outreach, and went relentlessly door-to-door to turn out voters who supported our candidates. Unions, particularly those who represent public employees, are exceptional at election-day turnout tactics. If a candidate wins by just a percentage point or two, it was frequently a ground game that pushed them over the line. If they lost by the same amount, you knew a stronger election-day get-out-the-vote effort would have won the seat. I was on the cusp of developing the Persuasion Matrix, and election work provided an intensive example of focusing on a desired action: getting voters to support your candidate. A clear desired outcome crystalizes tactics.

"I came to work in the labor movement because all the photo copiers work," one AFSCME staff person, Peter Schmalz, once quipped. Unions are among the rare progressive nonprofits that have the resources to do things well. Good pay and benefits meant they hung on to highly qualified staff whose knowledge of electoral politics and legislative processes was unparalleled in the nonprofit world.

For everything that AFSCME had to offer and teach me, though, my initial goal was to work for the Service Employees International Union (SEIU). As a reporter covering labor, I had been impressed with the SEIU's approach, and it was continuing to grow in stature with its nationally covered janitor organizing campaign and the strategic savvy of its president, Andy Stern. I had been at AFSCME for about 18 months when SEIU recruited me to lead communications for a new hospital-organizing project in Chicago. I was ready to go.

LESSON LEARNED

Understand your value at work, and get the salary that your abilities warrant.

15

The Right Message

Working people have precious few guaranteed benefits in the United States. Unlike nearly all other industrialized nations, employers aren't required to give paid time off for holidays or vacations, or breaks for employees during the workday, or paid parental leave, or extra pay for working overnight, or guaranteed pay if you get laid off—the list goes on.

Not coincidentally, employers have incredible latitude to thwart labor-organizing efforts. Employers routinely fire pro-union employees; it's illegal, but there are no consequential penalties for doing so. Employers can also interfere with and stall the union election process and inundate their employees with anti-union messages and scare tactics. In the most extreme cases, they hire union-busting firms who have these campaigns down to a science—the science of convincing people that a union would make their workplace problems worse.[1]

Unions, particularly the sophisticated ones like SEIU, use science, too. By the year 2000, SEIU represented more health-care workers than any other union—nursing home and home health care workers, nurses' aides, practical and registered nurses. But the path to getting enough density in the health-care field to raise wages and improve working conditions across the industry was through organizing large hospital systems.

SEIU set up the Hospital Organizing Project in Chicago in 2002. The effort was one of several national front lines to organize hospital chains—Tenet, Columbia, Advocate. My new job with SEIU was to lead communications for the campaign focused on Advocate Health Care.

Organizing in the traditional sense involves employees who want a union reaching out to their co-workers and getting enough of them to sign a petition to file for an official union election. But this approach—particularly when dealing with a large, wealthy, and powerful employer like a hospital—meant certain firing for employees who were organizing. SEIU's approach was to give hospitals somebody closer to their own size to pick on—a politically powerful labor union with nearly 2 million members. This strategy is called a "corporate campaign."

SEIU mobilized an intellectually and politically savvy group of staff and consultants to attack the corporation from every possible flank. Union researchers dug deep into Advocate, searching for vulnerabilities. Communicators polled to determine messages that could be most effective against the corporation. Legislative and policy staff looked into legislative initiatives that would challenge the corporation.

The goal was to get a neutrality agreement from Advocate. To get them to agree to do what collective-bargaining law required of them in the first place: not interfere with a union-organizing drive. Having a neutrality, or conduct, agreement in hand was the only responsible way to approach an organizing drive with a large employer. Without it, a union would be putting employees' heads on the chopping block.

We hired a polling firm to assess Advocate Health Care's image, to test which messages about the chain would most resonate and determine which messengers had the most credibility. We learned that Chicago-area residents were most disturbed by the possibility that people could lose their homes because of medical debt. They also reacted strongly to the idea that nurses believe their hospitals are understaffed, that hospitals have engaged in price discrimination against the uninsured, and that hospitals were miserly with charity care. Our polling identified then–state senator Barack Obama, US representative Jan Schakowsky, and then–Illinois attorney general Lisa Madigan as highly credible messengers. All of this background work helped us craft a campaign that would resonate with public and with political leaders.

This groundwork was expensive but critical. You cannot guess what messages will be persuasive or base your messaging on what most moves you: your boss or your board. To be certain of what messages work, you have to test them through surveys and focus groups with your target audience. Similarly, you can't assume who the most credible messengers are. You have to ask your audience who it is that they trust.

Knowing what a good sample of Chicagoland voters cared about, we started outreach to identify people who were deep in debt with Advocate Health Care. It wasn't hard to find them. We found people at risk of losing their homes or other personal, valuable items like wedding rings or cars. We publicized the hospital practice of charging patients without insurance a higher rate for services than those with insurance. Our growing cadre of grassroots spokespeople had stories and copies of hospital bills to illustrate every possible predatory billing and collection practice imaginable.

Our public activities resulted in a steady public drumbeat against Advocate. Rep. Jan Schakowsky moderated a panel of nurses talking about safe staffing levels. State senator Barack Obama introduced the Hospital Report Card and Discriminatory Pricing Reform Act.[2] Rogelio Guzman, who was in a car accident that nearly killed him, publicly spoke about how medical debt to Advocate bankrupted him and nearly resulted in losing his family's home. A Chicago alderman threatened to cut off free water to hospitals after a five-hour hearing that included a steady stream of horror stories from poor patients.

The headlines piled up:

"Uninsured Pay Twice as Much, $12,240 vs. $4,930 in Cook County,
    Union Study of Hospital Bill Finds"
Chicago Tribune, January 27, 2003

"Area Hospitals Bill Uninsured at Higher Rate"
Chicago Sun Times, May 26, 2003

"Sticker Shock: With Medicare and Private Insurers Getting Large Discounts,
    Hospitals Are Hitting the Uninsured with Huge Bills and Aggressive
    Collection Tactics"
National Journal, October 18, 2003

"Attorney General Investigating Hospital Charging Practices"
Daily Southtown, October 24, 2003

"Senate Panel Eyes Advocate's Billing"
Crain's Chicago Business, October 27, 2003

"Uninsured Patients Sue Advocate; Plaintiffs Decry Unfair Charges and
Aggressive Billing"
Crain's Chicago Business, November 19, 2003

As early as November 2003, Illinois hospitals agreed to adopt statewide, income-based discounts and to stop some aggressive collection
practices. As *Crains Chicago Business* reported (in the article just listed),
"By calling attention to an industry-wide practice of charging the uninsured as much as twice what it charges patients covered by health plans
powerful enough to negotiate discounts, the union created a groundswell
of support for new hospital policy." By January 2004, the trade journal
HealthLeaders did a cover story headlined "Under Siege: Hospitals Fend
off Hardball Union Tactics." They were feeling the pain.[3]

Two months later, the Illinois Hospital Association reached a legislative deal with SEIU that uninsured families with incomes up to $18,850
(the federal poverty level at the time) would get free care. SEIU had been
pushing a bill that would provide free services to anyone who made less
than $27,930 a year and require discounts for families making as much
as $75,400. The Illinois Health and Hospital Association, though, argued
that the higher limit was untenable for hospitals in poor areas. So we
compromised for the lower amount.

The legislative momentum continued, led now by another key SEIU
recruit from AFSCME: legislative director Bill Perkins. In the next state
legislative session, the Hospital Accountability Project crafted and passed
some of the most aggressive hospital legislation in the country: the
Hospital Report Card Act. With Barack Obama as the lead sponsor and
spokesperson, nurses across the state as public advocates, and dozens of
low-income families sharing their story of devastating medical debt, the
bill passed the Illinois State Senate and the House of Representatives
unanimously.[4]

The act required hospitals to publicly report on staffing levels, nurse
turnover and vacancy rates, and on rates of hospital-acquired infections.
This requirement gave nurses the information they needed to push for
better staffing, and it gave patients the information they needed about
quality of patient care. More than 10 years later, when I was serving
in the US Department of Health and Human Services in the Obama

administration, this legislation was still held up as a model for public accountability in health care.

But Advocate was not budging on a neutrality agreement. The union had invested heavily in the campaign, raised its profile in the state and among health-care workers, and passed important legislation. But we failed in our goal of winning an agreement that would allow us to organize Advocate Health Care staff. Slowly, we reassigned key staff and moved organizers to other campaigns. I moved on to become the communications director for the Illinois State Council and hired my deputy at the Hospital Accountability Project, Toure Muhammad, to direct communications at SEIU Local 1.

The corporate campaign approach had its successes. Notably, in 2003 SEIU won a conduct agreement with Tenet Health Care,[5] paving the way to major hospital organizing wins. When Tenet was in a battle with Columbia Health Care for new hospitals in Kansas City, it made use of SEIU's corporate campaign tactics. I was part of a strike team that dropped into Kansas City to create a load of public relations trouble for Columbia Health Care. We promoted one negative story after another about the hospital system, careful to have a range of spokespeople not associated with the union. Ultimately, local leaders decided that Columbia was too much trouble and that Tenet was the better future health-care partner for the city. Tenet had figured out how to make the most of its new partner.

The corporate campaign approach, though, can weaken over time. It's too far removed from the workers and their demands, and once journalists understand why you are attacking a specific company, they are not as likely to run with your stories. Nobody likes to be played.

Players, though, can recognize each other. Howard Peters, senior vice president of the Illinois Hospital Association, managed the hospital-side negotiations on legislation throughout the corporate campaign. At the end of the tumultuous Illinois legislative session of 2004, he asked me out to dinner—a surprising invitation. He graciously congratulated me on SEIU's victories, and said he rarely experienced having his head handed to him like he did this session. Might I consider coming to work for the

Hospital Association to lead their legislative and political communication efforts?

Getting an offer from a powerful campaign opponent is flattering, if flummoxing. Did he think this was all about effectively deploying tactics, to whatever end? I worked on this campaign because I believed we needed to create a level playing field for workers to organize. I also thought hospitals were frequently bad actors, more focused on profit than care.

I declined the offer. It's important to know your audience—the messages and messengers that move them. But it's also important to know yourself. Work on what you believe in.

LESSON LEARNED

A campaign can be effective on many fronts but still not be successful. David beating Goliath is a big deal because Goliath is more likely to win. And often he does.

16

Frontline Talkers

In the spring of 2004, a group of Chicago-area nursing home workers were about to negotiate their first labor contract. Everything about this process was new to these employees: working on committees to develop contract proposals and priorities, visiting elected officials, doing media interviews.

SEIU had successfully organized nursing home workers statewide.[6] Members had decided on which issues were most important to them. Sick days were a high priority; they had none. Of course their wages and benefits were also pitiful, but sick days were the focus of public messaging.

For any campaign—contract, legislative, political—SEIU always did spokesperson training for members. Members were the voice and face of the campaign, even though they often were uncomfortable with the role. At the first training I held for a group of nursing home employees on a Saturday morning, I did the usual: reviewed key provisions of what we were fighting for in the contract, making sure everyone was familiar with and could discuss the demands. But the interactions felt stiff. No one could relax enough to talk naturally. I certainly wasn't getting a sense of who would be good spokespeople—a key outcome of any training like this. I had to take a different tack.

"Tell me about your favorite patient," I said. Everyone smiled at once, many chuckled, some shook their heads. They all had stories. Usually, their favorites were the ones who gave them the hardest time. "I like the tough ones," one woman said.

A Black nursing home worker told the story of an explicitly racist white man she cared for. He gave her a hard time, and she gave him one right back. They ended up bonding over their shared irascibility and became unlikely friends.

The stories were pure gold. They demonstrated, more than any prepared talking point could, their professional and compassionate commitment to the people in their care. And they provided this care while making
barely over minimum wage, with sparse benefits and no sick days.

I respect research. I read the messaging studies; I look carefully at
polling about what messages work best. I let that guide overall messaging
strategy. But when you have grassroots sources, you always, *always*, get
out of their way so they can speak their truth. You never give them some
canned talking point that you tell them to memorize.

It is okay to tell them what *not* to talk about. You don't want them to
be hurt by sharing personal details in a public forum, and you don't want
them to compromise their credibility.

I worked with a nursing home employee who was an excellent spokesperson. Within an hour of working with her, though, I found out that she
had been married four times. After we had a couple sessions working on
her talking points—written from things she said that best reinforced our
contract demands—I went over the details she *shouldn't* share, such as her
multiple marriages.

Years later, when releasing research on youth homelessness at
Chapin Hall, one young formerly homeless woman with two small children shared many intimate details with me. She wanted to help others
by using her own story to emphasize the importance of preventing youth
homelessness. And she wanted to be clear about how horrible it was. I
understood her willingness to share that she traded sex for a place to live,
but I encouraged her to think long term, to think about what her kids
would read when they would search her name on the internet in 15 years,
and to not include what she wouldn't want them to see. She decided to
omit the worst details in her public statements.

Charlotte Ryan and Karen Jeffreys, writing about providing communications support for anti-domestic-violence campaigns, captured the
challenge of connecting people to the mainstream media. "Marginalized
populations' lack of access to the news media is not easily remedied,"
they said in a chapter of *Communication Activism: Media and Performance
Activism*.[7] "Using news media to engage in public debates requires skill
and infrastructure—resources rarely at the command of individuals.
Unorganized workers receiving pink slips do not issue media advisories

condemning their layoffs, for instance; similarly, domestic violence victims do not call press conferences. Hence, to gain access to mainstream
news media, marginalized voices need support from organized sponsors
with a communication infrastructure."

For working people, labor unions provide that infrastructure, albeit
for a shrinking proportion of them. And the media appreciates it. In my
experience working with reporters, they tend to be more forgiving and
generous with sources who aren't elected or in any way functioning as
official leaders. Journalists aren't trying to catch them making mistakes.
And they appreciate a good, authentic source and story.

With grassroots sources, you don't tell them what *your* talking points
are. You learn theirs.

The same year as the nursing home campaign, I learned that Katie, the
foster child who had lived with us the longest, had been shot and killed.

She was in Pearl, Mississippi, having traveled there with a truck
driver she had hooked up with. Katie's young adulthood had been tumultuous. As a kid, her compulsive behavior led her to fill her pockets with
coins and cookies. As a young adult, she found meth. Her three oldest
sisters had preceded her in addiction, but Katie's approach, characteristi-
cally, was more full throttle. She turned tricks out of truck stops to support
her habit.

I would only hear from the four girls who struggled with addiction
when they weren't using. They never tried to get money from me for
drugs, and they never stole from me. But they did reach out to me when
they had complicated problems to solve. Katie had called me nearly two
years before when I was working at the Hospital Accountability Project.
She was pregnant, and did not want to have an abortion, but was considering giving the child up for adoption. I researched adoption services where
she was living, and Jeff and I discussed the possibility of us adopting the
child. (Our son, Brendan, was four years old at the time.) Ultimately, Katie
decided to get clean and keep the child.

She made it through the pregnancy and the first few months of the
child's life before she started using again. The father took custody of the
child, and we lost track of Katie again until we heard of her death. We later

learned that she had been pounding on the door of the house where the truck driver's uncle lived and where she had been staying. The uncle was angry at the noise she was making, and he got his shotgun and shot right through the door and right through Katie.

In the few minutes she lived after she was shot, on the 911 call recording, you could hear her crying, "I just want to go home." I'll never know exactly what she was picturing when she thought of home.

Jeff stayed home in Chicago with Brendan, and I drove our minivan across Indiana back to Preble County, Ohio, where I first met Katie and her sisters and where she was to be buried. In a short eulogy I talked about the family therapy that Katie and I did together where we were taught to use "I" statements when things got difficult. You filled in the blanks: "I feel BLANK because BLANK and I need BLANK." Since this was a difficult as it got, my last words to Katie before her coffin was closed were "I" statements.

"Katie, I feel devastated because you are gone and I need you back."

"I feel scared because I might have to come here again, and I need your sisters to be careful."

"I feel guilty because I don't think I did enough, because I got tired, because I got angry, because I gave up, and I need you to forgive me for that."

After the short service, the girls were fussing over which of their male partners and friends were going to be pallbearers. But it was soon obvious who the six should be: the five sisters and me. Together, we carried Katie to her grave. She wasn't yet 25.

LESSON LEARNED

Everyone has their truth. If you are a communication professional working in advocacy, let the people most affected by an issue share their experience in their words. Provide training and guidance, but don't obstruct their truth.

17

Getting Votes for Barack

Union billboards have long been a fixture on the Illinois landscape. They salute labor union members who provide indispensable services or depict labor leaders who look to be 20 feet tall, evoking notions of disproportionate power. Big signs for big shoulders. There was little evidence, though, that such billboards did anything more than stroke the egos of the union leaders who were featured.

The Service Employees International Union has always prided itself on taking a different approach to communication. SEIU does lots of polling—testing messages, determining attitudes among segments of their membership, identifying nuances of voter sentiments in swing districts. Tactics are determined by this research.

So when I proposed a different approach to the union's campaign literature when Barack Obama was running for the US Senate in 2004, SEIU leadership was receptive. I was the SEIU Illinois State Council communication director at the time. We had worked closely with Obama when he was a state senator, designing legislation that would make hospitals more publicly accountable and relying on him to support better pay for home health-care and nursing home workers.

The primary field was crowded. Sen. Peter Fitzgerald (R) was retiring, creating a rare open seat with no incumbent to battle—an opportunity any ambitious politician watches for. Both Jesse Jackson and Carol Moseley Braun decided not to run, improving the viability of Obama's campaign. But lots of other people were running: 15 total, 7 of them Democrats. Union support was split. The American Federation of Labor and Congress of Industrial Organizations (AFL-CIO) backed Illinois comptroller Dan Hynes, while SEIU, AFSCME, and the Illinois Federation of Teachers supported Obama.[8]

Figure 1: The Persuasion Matrix

To get the Democratic nomination, Obama needed to stand out in this crowd. And he needed support from the rest of Illinois, referred to as "downstate" in Chicago. With more than 150,000 members across the state, many of them political activists who worked campaigns, SEIU needed to persuade its base to support "the skinny Black guy with the funny name," as he was frequently described back then.

By this point, my communication experiences and education were coalescing into the Persuasion Matrix model. I began using it to design campaigns that were highly strategic, with messages developed and channels chosen based on which specific populations we were trying to get to take which action. I led a working session with communication directors from each of the major locals, using this persuasion matrix to plan SEIU Illinois's approach to mobilizing its members.

Supporting Obama was the clear "desired action" in the matrix, but when we came to responding to the second question in this tool—who could do this desired action—we realized that we were talking about many different populations. That recognition only became clearer when we moved on to the next box to answer the question of why our target audience would campaign for Obama. The answer to that question would differ dramatically for a security officer in Rockford compared to, say, a nurse's aide on the south side of Chicago.

So we kept the desired action in the matrix constant but customized the "who," producing a chart for each of the following groups of members:

1. Nursing home workers
2. Security officers
3. Janitors
4. Home health care workers
5. Public employees

For the first time ever, we produced customized pieces targeted to each of these employee sectors. Mailers and talking points distributed to leaders addressed specific pieces of legislation and used specific quotes from Obama related to each group of workers. Nursing home workers learned that Obama championed an increase in state health-care funding that led directly to higher wages for nursing home workers. Home health care workers were reminded that Obama supported collective bargaining rights for them, which led to a 34 percent wage increase over four years. And so on. We examined Obama's legislative record and pulled out accomplishments that would most resonate with each segment of our membership.

The campaign had incredible momentum. Obama specifically urged African Americans to "put your shoulder against history and just nudge it a little bit."[9] But he inspired voters of all races. He got an assist from his opponents' shortcomings: billionaire Blair Hall's messy divorce and Dan Hynes's lackluster presence.

Ultimately, Obama won 53 percent of the vote in the primary and made a decidedly strong stride toward being the only African American in the US Senate.[10] It's difficult to measure the specific contribution that SEIU members made to his success, but parsing our communication based on a more precise understanding of our member audience was also a stride forward for Illinois SEIU. And we didn't buy a single billboard.

LESSON LEARNED

Moving people to act is hard. To be effective, you must segment your audience as much as possible and craft messages to address each group.

18

Campaign Blunder

About 30 John Kerry presidential campaign workers were bundled up in the Milwaukee Labor Center's parking lot looking up at the sky late on a Thursday night. It was October 27, 2004, and there was a total eclipse of the moon, also called the "Blood Moon" for its orangish-red color.[11]

At that point, I had been living out of a hotel in Milwaukee for a month. I was one of six Democratic National Committee regional communications directors, in my case on loan from the Service Employees International Union, working on Kerry's campaign against George W. Bush. I was building media lists, pitching stories, connecting local campaign activists to journalists, doing advance work for campaign events, picking up donuts and office supplies—whatever needed to be done.

Campaign work is relentless. From the moment you wake up to the moment you go to sleep, seven days a week, you are at it. You grab food on the run or hope for snacks to be delivered to the campaign office if you can't get out. The unyielding pace combined with the heat of battle leads to countless mistakes, from the professional (remember Dukakis in a tank?) to the personal (many a marriage has fallen to campaign liaisons). My monumental mistake in Wisconsin came from pure carelessness.

Getting media coverage for your candidate, especially if you are working with surrogates, is ridiculously difficult. Wisconsin's numbers were good in those final days of the campaign, so Kerry was spending time in more competitive states.

The Saturday before the eclipse, we had a rally featuring SEIU International vice president Eliseo Medina. Through a Milwaukee union steward, I had found an SEIU member, a local janitor, to introduce him and say a few words. We'll call her Rosa. She was an activist with the union, serving on the negotiating committee for her local's latest contract. Rosa was also active in electoral politics; the previous spring she had become a deputy registrar. I did no vetting of Rosa further than her recommendation from her steward.

In my advance press work for the rally, I quoted Rosa and Eliseo in the press release and put Rosa forward as a spokesperson. The rally went well with good member turnout along with all the campaign workers. But no media came, much to my disappointment. The next day Rosa told me that while she wasn't a US citizen, she was a documented permanent resident and could vote. She had even voted before she became a deputy registrar.

That's interesting, I thought, I didn't know that permanent residents could vote. Learn something new every day. That afternoon in the campaign office I mentioned this to Robert Kraig, the Wisconsin state council director for SEIU, who immediately reached out to the international for an official legal opinion. The opinion came swiftly and tinged with panic: only US citizens can vote. If someone voted who wasn't a US citizen, they did so illegally.

While no media had interviewed Rosa, I did have one conversation with a reporter from the *Milwaukee Journal Sentinel* about the possibility that permanent residents could vote. I called that reporter right away and told her that I had misunderstood something a member told me—it was a language barrier thing, I explained—and that you definitely had to be a citizen to vote.

When another reporter reached out regarding a story about SEIU's broader Get Out the Vote program, I quickly connected him with member sources throughout the country. I think he was stunned with my quick and thorough response. He didn't know how hard I was working to divert attention from my earlier screwup.

By Thursday, eclipse night, it looked like I had dodged a bullet. For once, to have a press release ignored by the media was a gift. Even now, nearly 20 years later, every time I think about how the story could have blown up as direct evidence of election fraud, by an immigrant no less, my stomach clenches and my hands start to sweat. Rosa did not intentionally vote illegally—someone had indeed accepted her voter registration—and SEIU wouldn't have encouraged or condoned voting by a noncitizen. If it had come out it would have hurt Rosa, the campaign, the candidate, and, undoubtedly, my career.

Five days in the final weeks of an election is an eternity. Fortunately, no one was thinking about Rosa, if they ever were. So, for the moment, out there in the parking lot, I could enjoy the Blood Moon with my fellow campaign warriors, unaware of Kerry's impending loss.

LESSON LEARNED

It's hard to stay on your toes when working long hours under tight time-lines. Know when you are most likely to make mistakes, and lean on your colleagues to spot you.

19

Authentic Voice

"Farm aid expenses eat away at donations; Only 28% of revenue from last year made it to farm families."[12] This headline was on the *Chicago Tribune* front page the day of Farm Aid's 20th anniversary in 2005. The concert, which has since become the longest-running annual fundraising concert ever, was in Tinley Park, just outside of Chicago. A colleague of mine, Rand Wilson, was managing communications for the event, and I had volunteered to help.

Negative news stories get communicators hustling like little else. We quickly consulted with Farm Aid administrators about how their money is managed, spent, and accounted for; looked into similar nonprofits and how their funds were distributed; and developed detailed background points to share with journalists. I emailed everything I developed to my friend for his use and then headed out to the concert venue.

Backstage—a huge parking lot—was a campground of luxury buses filled with prominent musicians. Dave Matthews emerged from one with his wife and two towheaded daughters. They shyly waved at Brendan, my own towheaded five-year-old who was along for the concert. Marijuana smoke billowed out of Willie Nelson's bus as the members of Los Lobos ambled out, smiling broadly as we all introduced ourselves. Willie's son Lukas, then only 16, had his own (smoke-free) bus and invited Brendan on board.

The atmosphere was not, by any stretch of the imagination, one of concern about a crisis to be managed. The huge press tent nearby was filled with journalists, the preconcert press conference about to begin. Here we go, I thought.

Neil Young walked up to the podium to open the press conference. He was carrying a copy of that morning's *Chicago Tribune*. He held it up.

"This is fucking bullshit," he shouted, adding, "the people at the *Chicago Tribune* should be held responsible for this piece of crap."[13] Then he ripped the newspaper in half.

The crowd roared. All talk was then about farmers, their foreclosure rates, the dangers of big agriculture, and what Farm Aid stood for and had accomplished in its 20 years.

"This is fucking bullshit" is not a talking point most communicators would recommend. But for Neil Young it worked. Now, other details were communicated—including that Farm Aid the foundation and Farm Aid the charity were two different bookkeeping entities and that the bulk of Farm Aid funds went to awareness campaigns, emergency relief, a toll-free hotline for farmers, and other programs. But Neil Young's approach, though unorthodox, was best practice for crisis communications: aggressively shut down the negative story and pivot to the positive story.

Most important, though, the response was authentic. Something Neil Young understands. In a *New York Times* interview, musician Kim Gordon reflected on a conversation she had with Neil Young. "One thing he said about singing—that it doesn't matter how good your voice is, as long as it's authentic—gave me a lot of courage and made me think about it in a different way."[14]

We can't all be rock stars, but we can all be authentic.

We loved living and working in Chicago; we had no plans to leave. Jeff went from serving as the executive director of the Illinois Death Penalty Moratorium Project to being the publisher of *In These Times*, a national weekly. At the Illinois State Council, though, I had access to those on a national stage, and that opened a surprising door.

In 2005, the same year as Farm Aid, SEIU won the first-ever national labor agreement with a home health care agency, Addus HealthCare.[15] The groundbreaking contract set higher standards for home health care workers while improving their wages and benefits. We announced the contract with a press conference in Chicago, which gave me my first opportunity to work with international president Andy Stern.

Stories that came out of that press conference continued to build the narrative of Stern's more nuanced, sophisticated approach to labor organizing. He was about leveraging the collective power of labor, yes, but building partnerships for better outcomes drove his strategy. If corpo-rate giants wanted national health care to reduce their costs, he'd work with corporate giants on national health care. Outcomes, not staying in opposite corners of a ring, were what mattered. It was an approach that attracted many, including me, but that put old-guard unionists on edge.

The different approaches to unionism came to a head later that year, when SEIU and the Teamsters broke away from the AFL-CIO, forming the unfortunately named Change to Win coalition.[16] That press confer-ence was also in Chicago, and I was managing logistics and some of the media relations. We opened every partition on our conference rooms at our Illinois Center offices on Wacker Drive to pack in dozens of journal-ists and TV cameras from all over the country and the world. I had never seen so much media in one room in my entire career. We found some boxes for Jimmy Hoffa Jr. to stand on so that he could be higher than the podium, and he and Andy Stern announced that SEIU and the Teamsters were leaving the AFL-CIO. Numerous other unions followed in the sub-sequent weeks.

Stern and I soon had another opportunity to work together. In 2006 he released a book, *A Country That Works: Getting America Back on Track*. Early the following year, I staffed him on the Illinois leg of the book tour. At one event he was stuck in a conversation with one of our contractors when he really needed to be socializing with members. I extracted him from that interaction. In another he was cornered by a woman who was desperately seeking a job for her son. I intervened, giving the woman my card and asking her to call me the next day, allowing Andy to move on.

As I was driving Andy back to his hotel room after the last event of the tour, he said, "If you ever want to work in my office in DC, know that there is a place for you there." I was surprised and didn't say much in response. But I remember feeling increasingly excited as I drove home. Barack Obama had just announced that he was going to run for president. It was 2007, and all of a sudden it looked like DC was the place to be.

LESSON LEARNED

Authenticity and confidence are a powerful combination. Find and deploy yours and see where this blend takes you.

20

DC Culture Shock

West Virginia University was only 200 miles from Washington, DC, but it may as well have been on another planet. In my 10 years in Washington, from spring 2007 until January 2017, I never met another WVU graduate. But I was surrounded by graduates of Yale, Harvard, Brown, and other Ivy League schools and elite liberal arts colleges. Andy Stern had graduated from the University of Pennsylvania, where he started his education at the Wharton School as a business major.

As soon as I started working at SEIU in DC, I could feel the culture shift. At first I thought it was a cultural difference within SEIU, but I came to learn that it was DC culture. Co-workers were competitors, and no hours were too long. The goal was to be, or appear to be, the smartest person in the room.

People actually talked like that. They said, "When person X and person Y are in the same room, I'm not sure who the smartest person in the room is." Almost always, persons X and Y were white men from middle- to upper-class backgrounds. They were groomed to think of themselves this way. I was not. I was as likely to think of myself as the smartest person in the room as I was to think of myself as someone with a tail or floppy ears.

This culture was intimidating but also perplexing. When I got to DC I had the advantage of being 47 years old with significant professional and life experiences. What was clearly valued in DC was not what I found most valuable. Working for Andy Stern, I was able to assemble teams from SEIU's large staff to carry out special projects. I looked for people who could *do* things. I sought out competence and dependability, not brilliance, though I frequently found the latter. And we did some powerful things together.

I still see, even now, a type of confidence among my friends from upper-class backgrounds that I doubt I will ever feel. Years ago, when I told my father I was going to the Soviet Union, he was upset. The fact that I would go so far afield scared him. "I know my place," I remember him saying, his voice heavy with emotion. He would later die in a house that was about 500 feet away from the house in which he was born. That was his place, literally. I may harbor an internalized notion of my place, as well, which keeps me from being as sure of myself in every environment. But I know that, even if I don't feel it, there are situations where I have to show confidence unwaveringly. In DC, every situation was that situation. No matter who was in the room and what advantages brought them there, my demeanor had to be driven by one thought: I know what I bring to the table, and I can deliver.

"It's hard to be special in DC." Early in my time in DC, I overheard a woman saying that to a young man who had just moved to the district. It was and remains a profound truth. The most special people are at the White House and on Capitol Hill and are literally the most powerful people on the planet. Then there are the key influencers in the for-profit and nonprofit sectors, like Andy. The rest of us are bit players.

But oh, what a show we all got to be in.

LESSON LEARNED

We all bring a unique set of experiences and skills to the table. No matter who is at the table with you, keep your strengths in mind.

21

Doing More with More

When Billy Bragg walked on the stage in Minneapolis on Labor Day in 2008, I was overwhelmed with relief. A capacity crowd of 30,000 people filled Harriet Island on a gorgeous day, and our week of intensive activity leading to SEIU's "Take Back Labor Day" concert was almost over.[17]

Bragg was the first performer because we knew he'd be on message. The British troubadour's entire career was a pro-labor message. Along with other musicians and union members and leaders, he participated in a backstage press conference and then began his performance while all of the journalists were still there working on their stories.

The Labor Day concert, with the Midwest swing state bus tour that preceded it, was the most complicated project I had ever managed. Between the end of the Democratic National Convention in Denver and the beginning of the Republican National Convention in Minneapolis–Saint Paul, SEIU sponsored a caravan through four Midwestern swing states to mobilize members to support Barack Obama. Seven days of intensive activity—including five press conferences, two large barbecues, and member meetings at every stop—culminated in the Minneapolis–Saint Paul concert on the same day that the RNC opened in that city.

The caravan included an SEIU-branded bus full of members from across the country. At each stop in Missouri, Iowa, Wisconsin, and Minnesota, we picked up more members to fill the bus, contacting media along the way. And we had "Barney" with us—a huge purple semitruck with the SEIU logo painted on it that housed the Mobile Action Center (MAC). Anywhere we stopped, members could board the MAC and work at one of the many call stations to encourage other members to vote.

SEIU understood how much it took to staff an effective communication project. I was managing this project out of the SEIU president

Andy Stern's office, but I had a dedicated communication director, Tyler Prell. Tyler oversaw a consultant to do all advance media work for each event, a consultant who managed daily YouTube releases, a consultant who managed blogger outreach, and numerous SEIU communication staff who supported members with talking points and statements. Yet another contractor managed the paid advertising buy to promote the concert specifically.

In addition to that communication team, we had staff managing the logistics of lodging, meals, and travel; Danny Goldberg, the former president of Mercury Records, managing the concert with Rose Presents, a Minnesota concert promoter; and Glenn Silber with Catalyst Media, who was producing short video clips to release as we moved along and filming for a documentary about the Take Back Labor Day project.

My project contact list of staff, consultants, and local contacts included 64 people.

About a week before the events were to kick off with the launch of the caravan on August 28 in Saint Louis, key staff and contractors were meeting at SEIU Headquarters in Washington, DC, to go over final details. We were 90 minutes into the meeting and had finished the agenda items, but we didn't feel done.

"Before we close, I want to ask everybody what they are most worried about," I said to the team. "Addressing those concerns will be my work plan for the coming week."

Permission to be vulnerable is rare in Washington, DC. Too often, your weakness is someone else's opportunity. That culture undermines teamwork. How can you function well as a group when you don't know what others on your team need?

As we went around the room, the atmosphere noticeably warmed. Each person shared what they were most worried about. We were able to solve some issues immediately; everything else was noted for follow-up. And everyone had a better sense of what others in the group were wrestling with and how they could potentially help.

I could play an attentive leadership role with this team because all details for the event were delegated to others. My job was to manage and support those others. Fully staffing a project allows a leader to lead. It also allows her the psychic space to make difficult decisions. This factor played out repeatedly during the project.

At a critical moment in planning the concert, for example, we had a fundamental difference of opinion between a consultant and a key staff person. Danny Goldberg, the former Mercury Records executive and a friend of Andy Stern, was understandably in charge of the talent lineup. He had secured some of the best usual suspects for a pro-labor event: Billy Bragg, Steve Earle, Allison Moorer, and Tom Morello (formerly of Rage Against the Machine).

Michelle Miller had an unusual job at SEIU. Her specific title was "member experience and creative programs for new media." She came to the union directly from getting a visual media degree from American University. She wasn't yet 30. She felt strongly that the lineup had to include hip hop. Goldberg said emphatically: no way. Folk and rock and hip hop have wildly different audiences. They don't belong in the same show.

I had to make a call: do I go with the experienced, highly credentialed consultant who had a relationship with my boss, or our own young staff? I had seen Danny be overconfident about numerous calls throughout this planning process. And for all of her youth, Michelle was in tune with the cultural zeitgeist. Besides, Andy Stern had recently called me into his office, annoyed with the prima donna behavior of our more eminent consultants. "You are on this project because I need an adult in the room. You are in charge," he told me.

I went with Michelle's recommendation, and the hip hop outreach began.

We secured Mos Def, and the Pharcyde—a combination of Imani, Slimkid3, Bootie Brown, Fatlip, and the Legendary Alternative Rap Collective. As it turned out, one of our most important bookings was Atmosphere, a Minneapolis hip hop band that drew a huge crowd and delivered the most energetic performance of the day.

A well-staffed project gave me the luxury of knowing my team members' assets and weaknesses, paving the way for good decisions.

Appropriate staffing also frees leaders up to manage unexpected problems. The first night that the tour participants gathered in Saint Louis, we were watching the Democratic National Convention in the Concierge

Lounge on the 29th floor of the Crowne Plaza Hotel.[18] Outside the large picture windows we had a beautiful view of the city and the famous Gateway Arch. But our attention was inside: we gathered for drinks, appetizers, and pizza specifically to listen to speeches by Al Gore and Barack Obama at the DNC.

In addition to SEIU staff, we had the first batch of tour participants. They were SEIU members from New York, Chicago, San Antonio, Kansas City, and several other places from throughout the country. They were all veteran political activists in the union. The excitement was a bit too much, though, for one member. He drank quickly and abundantly, growing progressively louder. The convention speeches were starting, but no one could hear them because he was being so disruptive.

No way, I thought, can we spend five days on a bus with this guy.

I gathered a few staff and SEIU elected leaders, and they agreed: he had to go. The one advantage of labor union work is that if you need a couple of big guys to remove another guy from a space, they are there and happy to do so. The member was escorted to his room and put on a plane first thing the next morning. I wasn't worrying about food or beverages for the event, so I could address the situation at hand. I didn't have to worry about how the guy was going to get home; our travel office took care of that. I just needed to make the decision that he had to go. And my team, having gelled so decidedly over the previous six months, was ready to mobilize to address the situation.

Over the years I have repeatedly seen lone communication staff held responsible for press coverage of their organizations—while also managing their website, producing brochures and annual reports, writing social media kits, and supporting internal communication. If an organization is not getting the visibility that it desires through earned media, it's rarely because any staff person is failing. With the very big assumption that an organization is doing something newsworthy, lack of coverage is almost always because no staff was dedicated to earned media.

Visibility was a primary goal of the Labor Day Bus Tour. We were out there to mobilize voters in swing states. In the Persuasion Matrix, that was our clear "desired action." Jo-Ann Mort from ChangeCommunications sat in the front seat of the bus with her stylish and enormous bag, from which she would pull a desktop's worth of office supplies: laptop, media lists, phone. After our kick-off press conference in Saint Louis, we moved on to press events in Iowa City, Cedar Rapids, and Madison. Earned media efforts were supplemented by a $140,000 local advertising buy spread across the markets we visited.

For five days Jo-Ann contacted journalists, ensuring coverage of each press conference, arranging for profiles of local members, mobilizing the entertainment media for the concert, and responding to every question and need a journalist threw at her. It was her sole job, and she earned us the attention we were looking for—including a lead story in the *Rolling Stone* on the day of the concert.[19]

In swing states where elections are typically decided by fewer than 3 percent of the electorate, every bit of mobilization matters. SEIU had thousands of members in these states. If they were excited by participation in this tour and concert, and that resulted in their persuading their family and friends to vote, it could add up to a decisive impact.

As it turned out, in three of these states—Iowa, Wisconsin, and Minnesota—Obama beat John McCain by more than 10 percentage points. In Missouri, Obama lost by a hair, 0.1 of a percentage point, or fewer than 4,000 votes. It turned out we didn't need Missouri to win, but with that narrow a margin a ground-game tweak could have changed the outcome. A couple more caravan stops in Missouri could have mobilized more members to call and knock on doors of their neighbors, friends, and family and say: "Vote for this guy. I know he doesn't look like you and he comes from a different place than you, but he will prioritize the needs of working people."

Nothing is more persuasive than a message about a candidate from a source a voter knows and trusts. Could 4,000 more people from Missouri have been persuaded to vote for Barack Obama? And could labor unions have turned them out? I think so.

LESSON LEARNED

Complicated projects require a well-coordinated team of specialists. When results really matter, do not scrimp on personnel.

22

To the Mine Workers

After more than a week of 12- to 14-hour days in meetings, forums, and press conferences at the United Nations climate talks in Poznan, Poland,[20] we were in for a treat. Bianca Jagger, easily the most glamorous environmentalist at the event, invited the International Trade Union delegation to dinner.

We were in a private room at a large restaurant off Old Market Square in downtown Poznan. The walls were made of small glass panes, like an old-fashioned greenhouse. At this point many of us had gotten to know each other through the hours of discussion and events. Wine and conversations were flowing.

It was December 2008. Barack Obama had been elected president but had not yet taken office. Labor delegates came to the UN COP (Conference of the Parties) Climate Talks from 32 countries, but, because of its new leadership, there was a particular buzz about the United States. Finally, all hoped, the biggest contributor to climate change might provide leadership to address it.

At the dinner, after at least one glass of wine, I was asked to say a few words. I am not a naturally strong public speaker. I'm also one to overprepare, but I hadn't had a chance to prepare at all. But I understood why I was on the spot. As a labor delegate, I represented the Service Employees International Union, one of the country's largest unions, with 1.9 million members. I was from the United States. And, like our host, I was a woman.

I decided to go right for the 800-pound gorilla in the labor environmental delegation: coal miners. They attended the climate talks but had a decidedly different perspective. They were against anything that curtailed the use of coal—an absolute necessity to address climate change—while the rest of the labor delegation stood with environmentalists on the need to phase out coal as an energy source. The mine workers did not socialize with the rest of the labor delegation after the daily sessions; they were not at the dinner. Still, though, between my own family history of coal mining and my five years spent in West Virginia, I had an affinity for the miners.

"I know that we can be frustrated with the mine workers," I said after a welcome and a thank you to Ms. Jagger.

> But we need to remember that for generations they sacrificed their health and their lives for cheap energy that we all benefited from. And they literally took bullets for the labor movement, leading some of the most aggressive and radical organizing campaigns in labor history.
>
> I'm not saying don't fight with them—they are wrong about the continued use of coal. I'm just saying that any solution to the climate crisis has to include restitution for and consideration of the people who did this work, their families and their communities. They are still our movement brothers and sisters, and no matter how much we might differ with them on the particulars right now, they still need to be treated as such.

"To the coal miners," I toasted. "And to all that they sacrificed."

I sat back down to warm applause, and the man beside me said, "The miners drive me crazy, but you just made me cry."

The UN Climate Change Conference happens annually, typically in early December. The year I went, it overlapped with my son's 10th birthday. It would be one of the longest stretches I would be away from Brendan, and I gave him a one-euro coin to hold on to that would be a token of sorts, symbolizing me and where I was.

On his birthday, he diligently put the euro in his pocket when he went to school, but he kept taking it out. He lost it and was completely distraught. His heart had completely accepted the symbolism of the coin; it felt like he had lost me. His attentive teachers at E.L. Haynes Public Charter School in DC helped him find it. He lost it again. More tears followed.

His father would soon pick him up from school and make things right again. But while I was having an unprecedented professional

experience—participating as a delegate to an international conference—
there was no avoiding my son having his own new experience: his first
birthday without his mother.

⊠

The best public-speaking advice I've ever received was to be yourself, just
more so. Small hand gestures get bigger, voice volume goes up, facial
expressions more . . . expressive. Like so much in good communication,
being authentic and telling a good story are key. If you are speaking about
an issue, find your personal connection to it and tell that story.

Earlier in that same year, March 2008, I attended the Green Jobs Conference in Pittsburgh,[21] my hometown. It was hosted by the Blue Green
Alliance, which was founded by the Steelworkers. I had written a speech
for my boss, SEIU president Andy Stern, on SEIU's environmental initiatives—initiatives that I was responsible for leading and coordinating from
his office. At the last moment, he couldn't attend. I was asked if I could
speak in his stead.

"Of course," I said. I mean how often does a speech writer get to
deliver her own speech? Since my father drove a coal truck throughout
the mountains that surrounded us in southwestern Pennsylvania, and
then ran a service station in a nearby neighborhood for decades, I could
also add my working-class, energy-related narrative to the beginning of
the talk.

Afterward, people didn't want to talk to me about our green contract
provisions or our member weatherization program; they wanted to talk
about my personal story. Similarly, when Van Jones, then the head of
Green for All, gave a keynote speech at the conference, what I most remember is him talking about his deceased father. I had met with Van
just the month before in his offices in Oakland to talk about what SEIU
could do to support his work. Later, Van went on to work in the White
House and then to become a CNN commentator. In Pittsburgh after his
speech, though, I remember going up to him and telling him how proud
his father would be of him.

No matter how much solid content you have to deliver, it's the stories
that make you a trustworthy and relatable source. And it's the stories that

people remember. So think about which of your stories illustrate what you most want people to know. Tell those well.

LESSON LEARNED

Identify the stories that best illustrate the point you want to make. Tell those stories well.

Part Four

School Reform

23

School Reform Origin Story

When I was a foster parent in Dayton, I used to visit Colonel White High School so frequently that the administrative staff in the office joked that they were going to get me my own school ID and jacket. I had one mission during my visits: to make sure my two foster daughters, Anna and Nora, one a freshman and the other a sophomore, were in the building. They had quickly figured out that the only thing they had to do to prevent triggering an automatic phone call home was to show up for homeroom between second and third periods. Then they could skip every other class.

When they weren't in school, they found dangerous places to spend their days. My neighborhood of Five Oaks, historically one of the few integrated neighborhoods in the city and where many of my friends lived, was much edgier than I had realized before the girls lived with me. Dayton was once the third-largest General Motors (GM) town in the country, after Detroit and Flint, but by the '90s plants were either closed or heading that way. While blue-collar jobs were declining, crack was emerging.

At the high school, no matter how many relationships I formed with individual teachers, it was impossible to remotely determine if my girls were in class; teachers were only required to take and report attendance at homeroom, and that's all they did. Without constant oversight, my girls were as likely to be in a crack house as they were to be in a classroom. As a result, it became too dangerous for them to live with me. Nora and Anna had to go back to their previous residential care placement in an adjacent rural county, where every child in care was carefully tracked in the small public high school.

This was my first experience of the real-life consequences of an underperforming public school. It was also the beginning of more than a decade of my K–12 activism that started when I became a foster parent, continued as my son entered Chicago Public Schools, and then became part of my union work with SEIU president Andy Stern.

After we moved from Dayton to Chicago, it was a relief to discover that there was at least a democratic system in place to hold schools account-able: the Local School Council (LSC). Each school has an LSC composed of community, parent, and school representatives. They have the author-ity to set policy for the school and, amazingly, hire and fire principals. In the spring before Brendan started school, I ran for and was elected to the LSC. McClellan Elementary in Bridgeport on the South Side was about 80 percent Latino/a and 10 percent white, with a few Black and Asian kids. It was nearly 90 percent low income.

I had already been to numerous meetings at the school before Bren-dan's first day in kindergarten. I learned in those months that the princi-pal was highly erratic, authoritarian, and sometimes cruel. She had been there for 27 years. She bullied people—parents, teachers, and students alike—publicly and relentlessly. As a Black woman who had authority at a school in a neighborhood that was not only historically white but also historically racist, she no doubt experienced ordeals that hardened her demeanor. But the demographics of the student population had changed dramatically. She was leading an underperforming school and doing so while intimidating and alienating parents and faculty alike.

The first day of kindergarten is always emotional. But it was oddly so for Brendan and me. In August 2005 we entered Ms. Brown's room at McClellan, just a block from our home. This was to be the first year that the kindergarten would switch from a half day to a full day, a major fac-tor in deciding that Brendan would attend the school. As the room filled with parents and excited and shy five-year-olds, a buzz started among the parents. Each parent was told, as we signed our child in, that instead of the full-day kindergarten that had been planned, it was going to remain a half day.

Parents were frantically trying to figure out what they were going to do now that their child would be done with school by noon. I knew that the classroom next door was empty—that's where we held our LSC meet-ings—so I called the room to attention and made my own announcement.

"If parents want to discuss this change and what we can do about it, please meet me in the classroom next door." (Brendan remembered this moment as me standing on the teacher's desk.) We exited the room and started gathering. It suddenly occurred to me that I hadn't even said goodbye to Brendan. I rushed back into the kindergarten classroom to give him a hug.

The parents introduced themselves, and we passed around a tablet so that we could write down our names and phone numbers to start a phone tree. The principal, we'll call her Dr. Jackson, pointedly closed the door to the room, making it clear that we were causing a disturbance. In the Persuasion Matrix frame, the desired outcome was clear: to have a full-day kindergarten immediately. Clarifying who could do it was the next challenge. Together, we talked about those we should reach out to. Everyone was going to call the local alderman, James Balcer. Several parents who didn't have to go to a job during the day volunteered to call school board members. My husband's cousin Norm Bobbins was on the school board and the president of LaSalle Bank. He was going to be my focus. That morning, many people were hearing about Dr. Jackson's last-minute decision to use money once allocated to full-day kindergarten on some other budget item.

We all dutifully picked up our kids at the half-day mark, which is when we learned that our calls had gotten results. McClellan's kindergarten would be full-day going forward.

Through the LSC I met very engaged and committed mothers who were already my neighbors and were to become my friends. Over time, we gained the confidence to use the full authority of the LSC. When Dr. Jackson's contract came up for renewal, the LSC refused to renew it. We began the long process of selecting a new principal for the school.

The Service Employees International Union, where I started working in 2002, conducted regular surveys of members to find out what issues were most important to them. In the mid-aughts, as Brendan was starting school, the quality of public schools was rising in importance for our members; for Latino/a members it topped the list, surpassing immigration policy. Simultaneously, charter schools were expanding and becoming a more common option, particularly in the low-income inner-city neighborhoods where many of our members lived. Hurricane Katrina also hit in 2005, devastating the city of New Orleans and its public school system, which eventually rebuilt as a charter system.

While SEIU members saw charters as a potentially higher-quality option for their children, political progressives saw them as a blatant attempt to undermine the power of teachers' unions and to divert resources into nonunion schools where teachers were paid less and had fewer protections. As usual, SEIU president Andy Stern had his own take. He saw charter schools growing, and he saw his own members' support for these schools. If charter schools were to be part of the public school landscape, the labor movement should figure out how to organize their staff. Andy frequently said of the United Auto Workers (UAW): "You didn't see them building all of those Honda plants 20 years ago?" Because the UAW didn't recognize a change in the industry or respond proactively, they lost density (the percentage of the industry workforce that was union). Stern saw the same thing coming for teachers' unions if they didn't work to organize charter school employees.

The labor movement has a lot of codes. Not crossing picket lines is the most visible, but among union leaders it was almost as egregious to cross into another union's territory—to organize and otherwise intervene with their workforce. But that's exactly what Andy started doing. When he hired me to work directly in his office in the spring of 2007, it was to manage special projects. Since SEIU represented nearly 2 million, largely low-income people, Andy thought we should be at the table for any major issue of the day, not just wages, benefits, and working conditions. Working as his direct senior aide, I had two issues in my court: climate change and school reform.

My first month working for Andy in DC, I attended a meeting that he organized at a hotel conference room near O'Hare International Airport in Chicago. He convened school reformers from across the country—but not teachers' unions. Among those in the room were Arne Duncan, when he was still at Chicago Public Schools and before he became secretary of education; Steve Barr, the founder of Rock the Vote and later Green Dot Public Schools; Russlynn Ali, of the Education Trust; Nadja Chinoy Dabby, of the Broad Foundation; and more than a dozen other prominent school reformers, with whom I would cross paths for years to come. Attendees were asked to not discuss the meeting outside of the room, so it was referred to for years as "the meeting that didn't happen." But it was where a lot got started.

At one point in this meeting, when the conversation was particularly tepid, Andy threw down a gauntlet: "When are you going to get your clothes dirty?" When are you really going to fight for the things you want to happen? I mean, really rumble? he was asking. Everyone knew that meant challenging the teachers' unions on the issues that were holding back genuine reform.

How exactly to do that became the focus of SEIU's tumultuous school reform work for the next two years. And I've got the dirty clothes to show for it.

LESSON LEARNED

Efforts to achieve social change can challenge relationships and require the sacrifice of sacred cows.

24

Thin Contract Persuasion

In 2007, when SEIU started dabbling in school reform and charter school organizing, nearly 1.2 million kids attended more than 4,000 charter schools.[1] Every year, the number was growing, with more than 300 charter schools coming online annually.[2] Cities like Detroit; Washington, DC; and Dayton, Ohio, already had more than a quarter of their kids in charters, while New Orleans—in the complete restructuring that happened after Hurricane Katrina—was at 70 percent and on its way to nearly 100 percent.

While much of the demand for school reform was broad and grassroots, conservative elected officials, business interests, and right-wing funders were driving too much of the change. We wanted to solve the problem of better schools for low-income families but not at the cost of substandard jobs for the people who work in the schools. Education reform was increasingly being built on a foundation of bad jobs.

The debate about charter schools was primarily framed as two options: One option is the traditional public school, which is large, centralized, and unionized. The other is the charter school, which is small, independent, and nonunion. But there could be a third way: schools that are independent, innovative, small, and effective for our kids—and union.

A key element in this third way was an alternative contract that allowed administrators and teachers the flexibility to take steps to improve school performance. Steps like lengthening the school day and hiring and assigning teachers based on performance not seniority. A contract with this approach, we thought, would better appeal to a new generation and type of teacher.

A team of SEIU staff, led by Jack Schutzius in the research department, worked with Green Dot Public Schools, one of the only charter

school group operators that was unionized, and other school reform partners to craft a model contract template to use in charter schools. This
"thin contract" was a radical departure from the lengthy and detailed contracts that characterized most school districts. The Los Angeles Unified
School District contract was more than 300 pages; the "thin contract"
template was 10 pages.

SEIU, together with New Schools Venture Fund, conducted five focus groups of teachers to test response to this contract. Focus groups
are an invaluable tool for understanding the nuances of an audience's
sentiments and reactions to messages. The information collected is qualitative and not necessarily representative of the larger groups of which
the participants are a part, but its richness can shape strategy in a deeper
way than polling can. The focus groups were made up of high-performing
teachers, such as Golden Apple Award winners in Chicago; teachers more
likely to end up in charter schools, such as Teach for America alumni;
and younger teachers just entering the field. Here are the major themes
that developed:

- Teachers did not defend tenure: Moving to a system of yearly contracts and elimination of tenure provoked little resistance and often strong approval. Even teachers who had tenure were ready for
  its elimination, seeing its key outcome as the protection of weak
  teachers.
- Teachers were flexible on retirement benefits: They could walk
  away from old-style pension systems in favor of portable 401Ks.
- Trade unionism did not draw these teachers to the job: Union
  membership was not a priority for these teachers. This priority reflected another survey that showed only 30 percent of new teachers
  think of their union as "absolutely essential."[3]
- Pay for performance was a sensitive topic: Teachers were skepti-
  cal that a fair and impartial system could be developed for basing
  pay on performance and were against using test scores for this
  purpose.

Armed with this thorough qualitative input, we continued to refine
the contract template.

While work on the thin contract continued, SEIU was also pursuing another strategy: establishing infrastructure for organizing parents to put
pressure on school systems. We provided $150,000 in seed money to
launch a "parents union" in Los Angeles, which had a bumpy start but
eventually evolved into Parent Revolution, which is still active today, more
than 15 years later.[4]

Over the course of a year, SEIU also worked to launch a more robust parent union organization in Chicago. Two key staff from the Broad
Foundation—Kevin Hall and Nadya Chinoy Dabby—worked closely with
me as we recruited and interviewed potential staff and built support for
the effort. As the primary funder of this effort, though, the Broad Foundation wanted sign-offs from Mayor Richard M. Daley's office and the office
of Chicago Public Schools superintendent Arne Duncan before proceed-
ing. We never got that blessing.

"Parents should be chaining themselves to the gates of these schools
and not leaving until the schools deliver for their children," Michael Bennett, then-superintendent of Denver Public Schools and eventually a US
senator, said to me in a meeting in his Denver office in the fall of 2007.
My SEIU colleague, Jack Schutzius, and Bennett's deputy, Brad Jupp,
were also in the meeting. We were there to discuss the thin contract.

Bennett, and everyone else working to improve schools, understands
the power of parents. It's unimaginable that a principal in an upper-mid-
dle-class suburban school system would decide on the first day of school,
as they did in my son's low-income inner-city school, that kindergarten
would be a half day instead of the expected full day. Parents with power
would have that principal's head on a pike.

There is considerable latent power in the massive number of parents
whose children are being failed by the public school system. Many of
these parents, though, don't feel like they can challenge established institutions. But if they were organized and supported to do so? The powers
that be were right to be nervous about a parents' union. This was power
that they may not be able to control. Ultimately, the Broad Foundation
pulled the plug on the Chicago Parents Union project.

Our meeting in Denver, though, had an unanticipated outcome. Brad
Jupp, who was Superintendent Bennett's senior academic policy advisor,

taught in Denver Public Schools for 20 years. He was active in the Denver Classroom Teachers Association and had been the architect of a merit pay pilot project. He was immediately taken with the thin contract template and wasted no time shopping it around.

Bruce Randolph School,[5] in Denver, educates almost entirely low-income students and was once considered one of the worst schools in the state. It came under the superintendent's control in 2002 and had been gradually improving. In November 2007, Jupp took the contract to a group of reform-oriented teachers at the school. "This is the kind of contract we need," they told him. They proceeded to modify it to their school and retitled it the "Professional Autonomy Agreement." By December they had won school board approval to waive their existing contract and adopt the new one.[6]

By the spring of 2008, we had turned the dissemination of the thin contract over to NewSchools Venture Fund, which planned to promote it through their funding of new schools. Andy and public-sector leaders at SEIU had been holding meetings with American Federation of Teachers and National Education Association leadership, pushing them to stay active in charter school organizing and alternative contracts so that they wouldn't cede union density in the K–12 sector. I had been working directly with Illinois teacher unions to push the same discussions, bringing them to the table on new charter school projects in the state.

In Denver the alternative contract model proved successful for Bruce Randolph School. Test scores improved, and the school was removed from the state's watch list. Subsequently, the category of "innovation schools" was launched in Colorado, and these schools were permitted to use the alternative contract. As of 2020 about a quarter of Denver schools were innovation schools.[7]

In the end, Andy decided he was done poking this bear. My work moved more toward SEIU's environmental activism and efforts to elect Barack Obama president. But the biggest benefit of my school reform work was yet to come.

Steve Barr, the head of Green Dot Public Schools, called me in 2009 to tell me about a student at Locke High School in South Los Angeles near Watts. Green Dot had taken over this failing school and turned it into four smaller schools. One student, Micheal McElveen, a rising senior when Green Dot took over, stood out in every way: as a student, as an athlete, as a positive young man who interacted effectively with others.

Micheal had received a full scholarship to attend American University and was moving to Washington, DC. Steve explained that Micheal was not only the first in his large family to go to college, but he had rarely been outside of LA. He's going to need some support in DC, Steve said. I reached out to Micheal, and we met for lunch across the street from the SEIU office on DuPont Circle. Conversation was pleasant and easy, and it was immediately evident how Micheal had gained so much respect. What was most memorable, though, was what happened after lunch.

When we came out of the restaurant, it was pouring down rain. "Wait a minute," he said, and we ducked into a covered space off the sidewalk by the Krispy Kreme. He took off his knapsack, pulled out a different pair of shoes, and changed into them, explaining that he had borrowed the ones he was wearing from another student because he didn't think he had the right shoes to wear to lunch. But he didn't want to mess up his friend's shoes in the rain, so he was putting his own shoes back on. The thoughtfulness and conscientiousness reflected in that single episode floored me.

Over the next couple years, Micheal became part of our family. Most important, he was a big brother and mentor to Brendan and many of his friends, with whom he had much more credibility than Jeff or I could ever have. When a smart, handsome young Black man from South Central tells a group of mostly Black teens that they need to lay low and stay off the streets to stay safe, those teens pay attention. Micheal ended up living with us for a couple summers, and then for a few months after he graduated from American and got his first job. Eventually, he asked if he could call us his godparents, since we were so much more than friends. I officiated at his wedding when he married his college sweetheart, and the couple eventually purchased a home near us in Chicago. They are family.

The school reform work touched our personal lives in another way. When we moved to DC, we dutifully looked up the best elementary and middle schools—Brendan was going into fourth grade at the time. We looked at the houses near these schools, and there wasn't a single house under $800,000 in those neighborhoods. We weren't going to any of those regular public schools. In the neighborhoods where we could afford to live, the percentage of students performing at grade level was as low as single digits; we simply weren't going to send Brendan to a school where only 9 percent of students were performing at grade level. But we wanted to live in the city.

We started looking into charter schools, and learned from some of my school reform contacts about Jenny Niles and her new charter, E.L. Haynes Public Charter School. It was preschool to grade 5, and each year it would add a grade all the way through 12th. We put Brendan on the waiting list and crossed our fingers that we wouldn't be stuck with the neighborhood elementary in Northeast DC where we lived. Four days before school started, we were notified that he got in. The school was then located in a few rooms above the CVS in Columbia Heights. Over the next few years, Jenny Niles and Haynes raised the money to build two state-of-the art school buildings, and Brendan eventually graduated from the high school in 2016.

In 2009 Andy Stern had announced his retirement. There were options for me at SEIU, but none of them were at the level that would justify my family's relocation to DC. I had applied for an appointment in the Obama administration but had no response as yet. My passion for school reform remained strong, so when the District of Columbia Public Schools, run by reformer Michelle Rhee, reached out to me to join its team as chief of staff over public engagement, I said yes. I was about to start the strangest single year of my career.

LESSON LEARNED

Focus groups, a powerful tool for refining your messages to targeted audiences, can influence your entire strategy.

25

Shoveling Message Manure

If you've gone to an old-school circus, you are familiar with the clown who follows the elephants and horses with a broom, entertaining and distracting the crowd while sweeping up the poop. Many a communication professional empathizes with that clown. Most of us, at some point in our career, have worked for someone who leaves a mess behind them as they go. And we're expected to clean it up.

DC Schools chancellor Michelle Rhee was the darling of school reformers across the country, and DC was seen as the best hope for turning around a major urban district. Her key reform building blocks included rigorously high teacher standards combined with capable central office staff. With more than half of DC students enrolled in charter schools, she was also working in an atmosphere of innovation with a plethora of new models on which to build.

In the fall of 2009, I joined DC Public Schools (DCPS) as the chief of staff in the Office of Family and Public Engagement. The month before I came on staff, Rhee had taken her most controversial action: she laid off 266 staff to address a projected budgetary shortfall. Before that, she had launched a process to determine which teachers added the least value to the school environment and had empowered individual principals to make the firing decisions.

Shortly after the layoffs were implemented, the chancellor did a phone interview with a reporter from *Fast Company* magazine. This reporter had written a profile of Rhee earlier, and she trusted him. It was January 2010 before what she said to him was posted. "I got rid of teachers who had hit children, who had had sex with children, who had missed 78 days of school."[8]

That statement sent shock waves through the school community,

128

particularly among those who had been let go. The already controversial job cuts became explosive.[9]

Senior staff, the press team, and attorneys from HR were brought together to clarify information about how many of the teachers were laid off for the serious infractions that the chancellor listed. Part of my job was to supervise the press team. The press secretary, Jennifer Calloway, and I drafted a statement with some follow-up questions and answers. We sent a draft of a statement to the chancellor, her chief of staff, and several other key senior advisors.

We decided to put the statement in the form of a letter to the city council chairman, Vincent Gray. Council members had asked for an accounting of her comments, and the communication shop had been encouraging more open and public communication with the city council. Addressing the council directly would acknowledge our accountability to that publicly elected body; releasing it publicly would get it in front of the community.

On Friday, January 22, the letter was ready. Nothing, though, moved to the media or to city council without the chancellor's explicit approval. At that time, Rhee required even the *Washington Post* education reporter, Bill Turque, to submit his questions in writing, and the answers were sent back in writing after extensive review. We asked for permission from the chancellor to move the letter to the city council and press. No permission came. Not on Friday, Saturday, or Sunday. By Monday, it had been four days of no response or clarification regarding one of the most inflammatory statements the chancellor had ever made.

On Monday, January 25, senior staff once again gathered around the chancellor's conference table and discussed what to do. I wanted to release the statement immediately—too much time had already gone by—but the chancellor decided not to do so. Instead, she chose to work with two people she could trust to tell the story the way she wanted it told: JoAnn Armao of the *Washington Post* editorial board and Tom Sherwood of the NBC affiliate in DC. Further, she wanted to wait until evening to talk to them so that other reporters (who had earned her wrath) couldn't get it for the next day's publications.

Rhee's play got the desired result on the editorial page. On Tuesday, January 26 the *Washington Post* published an editorial discussing her explanation of the statement.[10] In direct contradiction, though, a story by Bill Turque on the front page of the Metro section said that yet a fourth day had gone by with no explanation of her comments.[11] Rhee continued to look bad regardless. But the *Washington Post* looked even worse. Rhee, an outside player, ended up provoking a public display of internal tensions at the *Post* by instigating conflicting stories on the Metro page and the editorial page. The woman had a gift.

In follow-up coverage of the incident, Rhee was asked why Turque didn't get the information when the editorial page did. It was her communication staff's fault, she said. They had botched the release, she said, blaming the clowns with the brooms.

Before the bloom started coming off of Rhee's rose in 2010,[12] her reputation as an aggressive and effective reformer drew talent from across the country to DC Public Schools. Predominantly young, smart, passionate school reformers were drawn to the mission of transforming a major public school system. Many of them Teach for America alumni and graduates of some of the most prestigious schools in the country, they were convinced that if they could recruit high-level teaching talent for every inner-city classroom, public education would be transformed.

This talent-magnet was as evident in the communication team as it was in other central office departments. Everyone in this shop had arrived since Rhee began. A few months after I started, Press Secretary Jennifer Calloway moved on to another position and was replaced by Safia Simmons, who was initially less confident but equally talented. (She went on to be Rep. Elijah Cummings's press secretary.) Katie Test served in the role of communications coordinator and was the department dynamo, bringing 110 percent of her energy and project management skills to the dozens of new communication tactics we hatched. Fred Lewis brought a reliable steady hand and good humor, while Nicole Smith's smart, youthful passion and incredible work ethic lifted the whole shop. I loved this team.

They were also all dedicated learners. As I did with any communicators I supervised, I introduced them to the Persuasion Matrix and talked to them about the principles of persuasion and the importance of clarity in communication goals. The first two questions you always need to answer are: What do you want to happen? And who can do it? All tactics should flow from the answers to those questions.

National media coverage, including the *Washington Post*, was a distraction that frequently worked against our communication goals. The communication shop was more focused on reaching families and faculty in the effort to bring them along in the school reform effort and improve student performance. We started numerous new targeted communication channels, from Facebook groups, to Twitter chats, to focused newsletters. Over six months in 2010 our monthly "touch points" to our audiences went from 12,000 to 73,000. We leveraged targeted newsletters, public events at parent resource centers, and social media to get our messages out. Katie Test led many of these efforts, bringing strategic skills that she continues to apply in her own PR firm, Forthright Advising. The entire team put in long hours staffing evening and weekend events where we could communicate with families in person.

Rhee's notoriety did make the media want to cover DCPS to an unusual degree, though. Of the 12 stories we pitched to the *Washington Post* in the first five months of 2010, they did 9 of them. While Rhee's relationship with Bill Turque, the *Post*'s education reporter, was in the tank, my relationship with him was improving. We started regularly meeting for breakfast.

Rhee's signature management tool was the "school stat." At these regular meetings, senior staff from a department would be seated on one side of the chancellor's conference room table, and the chancellor and her "chiefs" were on the other side. Hours of effort were put into painstakingly prepared presentations. Two of the chancellor's staff were assigned exclusively to work with departments to prepare for the school stats.

The teams would have 30 minutes to present, discuss, and defend their recent work, and frequently there were two or three school stats consecutively. And while Rhee was flanked by all of her top deputies, their role was limited to occasional follow-up questions and points of information. School stats were all about Rhee.

Typically, slides that showed improvement and problems solved were quickly passed over. Under Rhee, doing things well was expected and not worth comment. Even if the department heads sitting across from her tried to publicly acknowledge the good work of their staff in the room, Rhee would impatiently wave them along.

School stats were fascinating, stimulating, and painful. And they were the hottest ticket in the office. No matter what time school stats were held, you could count on a full house. Staff coined a name for the roughest sessions: "slaughter stats." Senior staff on the hot seat across from Rhee would not only be challenged on content but also be told, in Rhee's two favorite adjectives, that what they were doing was "crazy" or just flat out "sucked." All of this in a room filled with dozens of junior staff and even interns. Some of these slaughter stats became legend—in the office and, too frequently, in the community.

In May 2010 it was the Office of Family and Public Engagement's turn for school stat. Our activities and channels had greatly expanded since our last school stat. We had five targeted newsletters, a new Twitter account, and growing Facebook pages and parent email and phone lists. Website views were up 42 percent. (Weeks after the school stat, DCPS won an award for the best K–12 website in the nation from the Digital Education Achievement Awards Program.[13]) We worked to quantify and summarize this progress and were excited to present our results.

An hour before school stat began, I was notified that we were to start with the slides about media coverage. We had compiled a detailed chart about our most positive and negative coverage. The positive coverage was strong: rising test scores, increased graduation rates, reaching a tentative agreement with the teachers' union, becoming a finalist in the federal Race to the Top grant competition. They were virtually all Rhee administration accomplishments that we had pitched.

The negative coverage was driven by the previous October's reduction in force, a controversial leadership change at Hardy Middle School, the *Fast Company* comment, and the public conflict between Rhee and the city's chief financial officer. With the exception of the staff cuts, DCPS's negative headlines were a direct reflection of Rhee's combative relationship and careless media interactions. The content of the media analysis projected on the wall at that moment made this abundantly clear, and Rhee's response was immediate and emotional.

"Your media work sucks," she snapped, interrupting me. "You're trying to pitch positive stories and nobody cares. You're pitching all the wrong stories." The next slide was a detailed analysis of our story pitches and how many of them landed. Since Rhee cared most about the *Washington Post*, those were pulled out separately, demonstrating how many of our pitches resulted in stories.

She did not want to look at that slide, or any others on the media. The reality was that we could get positive features and stories placed nearly daily on good things going on in DCPS, but they were a blip on the media radar compared to the ink and the airtime one of Rhee's public conflicts would bring.

We moved on to other topics: web usage growth, community engagement, parent work, volunteer recruitment. But none of it was of any interest to her. And as she was in slaughter stat mode, the rest of her team went quiet, as they typically did.

The public engagement team was demoralized. Those who worked on the slides that showed accomplishment across the department were affected by Rhee's lack of interest in their work. Those who had put in long hours doing a level of communication work that was unprecedented at DCPS—including aggressive media outreach—were devastated. I felt that I had failed to defend and fight for the accomplishments of my team. Days of fraught conversation and résumé updating followed.

School stats were good theater, but under Rhee they were bad management. Throughout central office, staff who were most eager to leave were those with a strong sense of their own value: those who knew that good work and dedication warranted respect, acknowledgment, and reward. They could live with nearly four years of no raises, but the strongest among them had little tolerance for emotional mistreatment and disrespect. On Rhee's team, it wasn't the survival of the fittest; it was the exodus of the fittest.

That May slaughter stat was the beginning of the end for the strong central office communication team.

LESSON LEARNED

When managing people, critique in private, praise in public.

26

Cutting Turf for Toddlers

Miriam Calderon was among the most indomitable of the talented leadership drawn to DCPS during the Rhee era. She led the early education team, which had achieved dramatic growth in the early education program. In 2010 alone they added 25 new preschool classrooms across 18 schools, serving 700 more students than the year before. They were driven by the belief that what they did for these three-year-olds each year would have a direct impact on how many high school graduates DC would have 15 years later.

The large influx of early ed students in August 2010, though, presented challenges. Calderon wanted to be sure to allow teachers and staff time to do thorough assessments of each child during the first week of school. To do that, they needed to start in smaller groups.

Calderon shared a "staggered start" idea with Rhee, explaining that children with last names that began with A–L would come the first two days, and those with last names beginning with M–Z would come the third and fourth days. Rhee supported the plan but needed assurance that every family would be notified. Applying the Persuasion Matrix, we found the desired action was clear: a strong school year start for preschoolers. And the first people needed to make that happen were the parents of the preschoolers. When Calderon and her staff came to me for help on this communication effort, I told her the only reliable way to reach a low-income, low-literacy population is to knock on each of their doors and talk to them. Her team didn't blink.

The early ed team formed an "Innovation Team" for anyone who wanted to help address this challenge of visiting up to 4,000 families with preschoolers. In August. In sweltering DC.

Over the next months we talked to labor union field directors and

Obama campaign organizers and found everyone in central office with any political campaign or canvassing experience.

This cross-department team learned everything they could about cutting turf, walk routes, at-the-door scripts, likely number of contacts per hour, and canvasser safety tips. They decided that they'd deliver a small gift for each child—a book—and found a group to donate them. The DCPS Office of Youth Engagement wanted to participate to communicate about immunizations. They merged their data with early ed, making it possible to have each child's immunization information on the walk sheets. Canvassers could give families information about how to update their children's immunizations before school began.

On the weekend of August 14 and 15, more than 50 central office staff and other volunteers gathered at ward bases throughout the city, checking in with their "ward captains" for doughnuts and walk sheets. They fanned out across the city.

In our training role-plays the day before, we practiced how to deal with hostile and confrontational parents and families. We wanted everyone to know how to manage difficult situations in a way that would de-escalate conflict. But those situations didn't happen.

In follow-up conversations and surveys, staff spoke effusively about the powerful conversations they had with families. Staff were trained not to enter people's homes, but many found it impossible to turn down invitations, finding themselves in lengthy and intimate conversations around kitchen and coffee tables.

Often families were initially cool and suspicious when someone they didn't know asked about a preschool child by name. And it was usually a white person inquiring about a Black child. But then they were handed over a book for the toddler and assured that the canvasser was just there to make sure the child got a strong start in the first couple weeks of school. Coolness and distance often became surprise followed by genuine warmth.

"You're really going to every family's house?" I was asked as I canvassed.

"We're going to try," I replied.

"God bless you."

From these families we learned about everything from potty-training challenges to neighborhood dangers, from housing values to new grand-babies. This was no political canvass. This was intimate. And it was effective: the first week of school had unusually high attendance for pre-schoolers. While the message and the messengers are important in any communication campaign, this campaign showed the channel—door-to-door canvassing—could be the key determinant of success.

LESSON LEARNED

Door-to-door canvassing is a uniquely powerful outreach tool that can be used to build trust and participation in public institutions.

27

Cultural Incompetency

Who needs to be on your side for your organization to be successful? The answer to that question is key to any successful communication strategy. Every group or individual on the list of necessary allies needs careful attention. If the desired action in the Persuasion Matrix is to sustain community support for school reform efforts, you need to understand that community well enough to move them to actively support your mission.

In the District of Columbia, many long-term residents view themselves as living in a colony that is subject to the whims of powerful outsiders. Historically, DC was majority Black, with a predominantly white transient political class. It wasn't until 1975 that city residents got to elect their own mayor. Before that, a three-member board of commissioners appointed by the president ran the District. DC still has no vote in Congress.

In no other city does "I was born here" carry more local political weight. And few populations are more suspicious of a group of people from elsewhere coming to "help." Changes in the school system are particularly sensitive. Generations of families attended and feel deep attachment to virtually every local school. Experimental reforms or restructured or closed schools are potentially explosive events. In DC, school reform is personal.

DC Schools chancellor Michelle Rhee did not have the trust of the community. Her major strategic error, though, was that she didn't think she needed it.

On February 1, 2010, the results of a new poll were released that showed a dramatic drop in both Rhee's and DC Mayor Adrian Fenty's approval ratings.[14] Among African Americans, who made up 80 percent of the school system, Rhee's approval rating had fallen to 28 percent. It was the third year of Rhee's tenure and an election year for the mayor.

After years working in labor and politics, I knew a poll like this meant immediate crisis communications and longer-range strategizing. I rushed to get into the office early. On my way to the train I was handed the free *Express*, which featured a huge photo of Fenty and Rhee with a 200-point-plus headline: "United they FALL." I was the first one in, and, expecting a meeting to be called, I checked my email. I started drafting some re-sponse tactics and talking points as others started arriving at work. I could hear everyone greeting each other and chatting normally—as if nothing had happened.

I checked in with our two young legislative staff who worked directly with the DC Council and who had worked on Fenty's mayoral campaign. They, too, were awaiting instructions. So I went to the chancellor's office, where I was met by her chief of staff. There were no plans to comment about the polling, she said. We expect to be unpopular because we are the ones making the difficult decisions, she elaborated. Despite a dramatic drop in our approval among the people we were ostensibly serving, we made no attempt to address their concerns.

Rhee repeatedly told audiences and journalists that she didn't care if people liked her. But what listeners heard was that she didn't care what they thought—about her or about how she did her job. Accountability to the city council, for example, was handled as a tedious exercise in suf-fering fools. Anyone attending, watching, or covering those city council meetings could see that. The lesson wasn't lost on the voting public.

Rhee's independence from public opinion was a point of pride for her, an indication of her purity of purpose. But for the public engagement office, it meant certain failure. If you don't care what others think, why be transparent with the media? Why care if your community meetings are poorly executed and sparsely attended? Why invite community partners and leaders to be a part of the reform? Why address the overflowing boxes of returned mail that indicated our parent mailing lists were in lousy con-dition? Why do outreach or communicate at all? The Rhee team thought they needed no one else to be successful. They were wrong.

Years before, in a meeting of SEIU leaders, then-president Andy Stern was questioned on the lengths we were going to support a candi-date. "You can't govern if you can't get elected," he responded. I thought of that often at DCPS, with the additional caveat that you can't get elected if no one likes you. It *did* matter if people liked Michelle Rhee. Nationally, many in the school reform movement saw a smart and bold leader. But locally, parents and city leaders saw an imperious outsider who demonstrated little respect for the community she served.

Cultural sensitivity starts and ends with that respect. In 2010 a harsh lesson was delivered about the consequence of not paying that respect.

The many, monied national players in school reform who wanted Michelle Rhee to succeed were willing to make endless resources available to her. This included top-level public affairs talent. Not long after the devastating polling in early 2010, Anita Dunn was brought on as a consultant. She was President Barack Obama's first communication director and a principal at SKDK (she is the "D").

Hard charging, quick thinking, and no nonsense, Anita was, and remains, the most strategic and competent communication professional I have ever known. She and I would talk on the phone every morning at 9 a.m., mapping out that day's media strategy and longer-term communication efforts and clarifying talking points. What actions and soundbites would counter negative images and build positive ones? What outlets could we get those into? Which high-profile journalists are working on education stories, and can we get any of our successes into those stories?

Rhee was in constant demand for interviews nationally and internationally. We once had a Korean TV station following her around for a week. TV talk shows loved her because she was attractive, smart, and pithy in a relentlessly biting way. But what was good entertainment value for the media was frequently not good for DCPS, or for Rhee herself. Daily briefings on carefully crafted messages were no match for her own proclivity for tactless pronouncements about the causes of public school failures. She saw herself as a truth teller, and no professional communication advice was going to slow her rhetorical roll.

Rhee's style proved professionally fatal to both her and her boss, Mayor Adrian Fenty, who lost the September 2010 democratic primary to Vincent

Gray. Rhee, in a realistic acknowledgement that Fenty and his office was her sole support, announced her resignation a month later.

The communications team knew it had a challenge in framing Rhee's departure, but we also saw an opportunity to move to a more positive tone. We would not miss the distraction of Rhee's caustic public personality.

Right after her resignation, I pitched a city council outreach strategy to a senior staff person. I was asked which member of my team I most trusted to carry it out. "Katie Test," was my immediate answer. "If that's your best person, she's the one who should do it," I was told. At the time, I was optimistic that my team's talents could be put to more proactive use going forward.

But while Rhee was gone, her loyalists remained. I knew my organized labor background made me suspect to many on this reform team. My push for a different approach upon her departure was increasingly seen as evidence that I was never genuinely part of the Rhee team.

In November, just a month after Rhee resigned and just before Thanksgiving, the chief of staff called me into her conference room at the end of the day. "Look," she said. "It just doesn't work to have a key communication person be at odds with the leadership's approach." It was time for me to go. They would keep me on the payroll through January, but I was to leave immediately. The next day they had delivered the same message to Katie Test. I was certain that the question just weeks before about the person I most trusted was to get me to point to my most loyal staff person.

When I got home I called Anita Dunn. It was the night before Thanksgiving, and she was hosting a large family gathering the next day. She was stunned when I told her that they'd laid off Katie and me. With pots and pans clanging in the background as she prepared for the holiday meal, she expressed her alarm, dismay, and appreciation for our work together. And then she said: "I guarantee you will be happier in your next job."

She made good on that guarantee.

LESSON LEARNED

You don't need everyone to love you, but you always need other people to be successful.

Part Five

The Obama Administration

28

Persuasion and Obamacare

The Affordable Care Act (ACA) didn't transform the US health-care system. But the 2010 passage of what was later dubbed Obamacare did provide a path to health insurance for millions of people—a path that was
dependent on a massive communication campaign to persuade people
to enroll.

I joined the Obama administration shortly after leaving DC Public
Schools. Anita Dunn, Obama's first communication director, whom I
worked closely with when she consulted with DC Public Schools, said
that the US Department of Health and Human Services (HHS) needed
experienced communication leaders to manage ACA outreach. And, after my fiasco with DCPS, I certainly needed a job. True to her word, she
hustled my resume through the Presidential Personnel Office, and by
the end of the multistep interview process I had my pick of five possible
positions, including communication director at the Centers for Medicare
& Medicaid Services, press secretary for the surgeon general, and public
affairs director at Administration for Children & Families (ACF). When
I learned about the dozens of programs that ACF oversaw, there was no
question where I wanted to be. The agency encompassed most of the
human services work of HHS: child welfare, refugee resettlement, early
childhood programs, programs supporting low-income families. It was a
natural fit not only with my advocacy for low-income people while working at the Service Employees International Union but also with my foster
parenting and work in public schools.

ACF's communication campaign about the ACA began with extensive census data about who was uninsured in the United States. We knew
what geographic areas the uninsured were concentrated in and what type
of work they were more likely to do. And we knew that a large portion of

the uninsured were already enrolled in at least one federal benefit pro-gram. ACF served millions of Americans through dozens of programs: childcare, child support, foster care, Temporary Assistance for Needy Families, Head Start—more than 70 distinct programs in all. I worked with each major program office to develop a strategy to reach the people they served with news about available health insurance and how to enroll. We knew that signing up for health care was difficult; the complexity of coverage options was overwhelming if not incomprehensible. The unin-sured needed to work with health-care navigators who could help them through the application process. Connecting our beneficiaries to naviga-tors was a primary goal of our outreach.

With the leadership of each program office, we filled out the Persua-sion Matrix. The "desired action" for each office was to get program par-ticipants to enroll in health care. Some were straightforward. The Office of Child Care managed federal childcare subsidies nationwide for low-in-come families. When we identified that it was the state childcare offices that administered this program, we developed materials and resources for them to use to connect those receiving childcare benefits with health-care navigators to help them get health insurance. We did the same with the Office of Head Start, supplying the program's social workers with ap-propriate outreach materials.

This strategy work got even more complex with the Office of Com-munity Services (OCS). One of the programs OCS administered was the Low-Income Heating and Energy Assistance Program (LIHEAP). When we did the matrix for this group of benefit recipients, we had a major breakthrough at the "messengers and channels" step. We realized that the one messenger, the one channel that reaches all the people who were uninsured—indeed that reached into every home in America—was utility companies. This insight was a strategic breakthrough that would drive our outreach strategy into the second term of the Obama administration.

Communications work with each program office was tempered by know-ing the Supreme Court was going to rule on challenges to the Affordable Care Act. If the law was struck down, our work would be for naught.

On June 26, 2012, about a dozen of my colleagues were in my office at

Figure 1: The Persuasion Matrix

what was then called the Aerospace Building near L'Enfant Plaza, where ACF was located at that time. We had gathered to await the Supreme Court decision on the ACA and were watching CNN on the large TV mounted on the wall. While my colleagues sat mostly around the conference table, I sat at my desk with Bloomberg's SCOTUSblog up on the screen, refreshing constantly. Everyone else in the room let out an audible moan when Wolf Blitzer announced that the law had been struck down. I was the lone person cheering, since I was seeing on the SCOTUSblog that it was upheld.

I was later to find out from HHS secretary Kathleen Sebelius that President Obama was learning about the decision in the same flawed way that we were. He was in the situation room in the White House when the decision came down. He walked out and looked at CNN on the screen on the wall, which had a crawler saying the law was shot down. "It's down," Obama said. "No, it's up," came a reply from a nearby room where someone was monitoring the SCOTUSblog. They went back and forth that way for a few minutes. Then CNN made the correction: the law was upheld.

Devastation followed by confusion and then elation. This sort of roller-coaster ride was one reason that serving in a presidential administration was so exhausting. The Supreme Court decision laid the groundwork for launching the Affordable Care Act marketplace in 2013. After that, our outreach intensified.

When we decided to focus on utility companies, we went back to the Persuasion Matrix, inserting a new desired action in the top square: getting utilities to help their customers enroll in health care. The message: The number one cause of personal bankruptcy is unexpected medical expenses. Bankrupt people can't pay their utility bills, so help us help them avoid unpayable health costs by getting health insurance.

Then we did a matrix for each company, figuring out how to reach them, those in the company we should approach, which messages would be most persuasive. Because of the high level of uninsured in Texas, Florida, and the Mississippi Delta, we started in the South. We reached out to Atmos Energy in Texas, Entergy in Louisiana, and Florida Power & Light. Entergy already had a robust outreach program to its low-income customers and was all in. For years they had helped their customers sign up for food stamps and other benefits, all with the goal of putting them in a better position to pay their utility bills. They happily incorporated our materials into their mailings and allowed ACA navigators to set up tables at their energy fairs.

Atmos in Texas and Florida Power & Light, though, gave "Obamacare" the cold shoulder and gave us a brusque "no thank you." We turned our attention north, where there were large pockets of uninsured in more politically friendly environments. We thought we might do even better with a publicly owned utility, so we reached out to Philadelphia Gas Works. They were instantly responsive. I was soon on an Amtrak train from DC heading to a meeting with their senior management. They not only set up places for navigators to work in all of their offices in low-income areas but also publicized the effort, which led to news coverage of this utility-focused initiative for the first time.

It was quite a surprise to see a tweet from the White House in January 2016 calling attention to the Philadelphia Gas Works partnership on ACA outreach. Internal communication among the vast network of political appointees was so dismal that news coverage and social media were frequently the only way we knew what other appointees were doing. Each year we would watch the State of the Union address for announcements about our programs. Did the White House communication staff ever even wonder how the utility partnerships came about? I would never know.

As we continued to reach out to utility companies, we got better at refining messages that would land with their senior officials. Maps were particularly helpful. With regional census offices as our partners, we were able to produce maps of where the uninsured were, by census tract. Utility companies, we learned, were particularly cagey about talking about turning off power to those who hadn't paid their bills. No law required them to disclose how frequently they did this and to whom. But they knew in great detail where the bills weren't paid. And they knew how bad they would look if the public saw exactly whose plugs they were pulling.

That's why the maps resonated. In February 2016 we met with six executives from Detroit Power and Light (DP&L) at their headquarters. Two women from the Detroit Health Department and a representative of Enroll America in Michigan joined me and Angela Green, the ACF regional administrator based in Chicago. We handed out a map showing where the uninsured people were in Detroit specifically, and the health department officials emphasized that these were the same areas that had the highest incidence of asthma, heart disease, and infant mortality.

As they took in the map, we saw the DP&L officials look at each other. "This looks familiar," DP&L vice president Nancy Moody said. We knew they were also looking at a map of where their most frequent shutoffs were.

DP&L agreed to work with us on targeted outreach to the mapped areas in Detroit. They did not want our partnership broadcast, particularly to the rest of Michigan, which was considerably more conservative than

Detroit. Most important, new relationships were established between state health department officials and a utility company with more than 2 million customers.

"If you build it, they will come," was a compelling line from the movie *A Field of Dreams*. If only it were so. Here's the real-world math: if you build it, figure out who is most likely to come, determine the best messages to get them to come, find out who the most persuasive messengers will be to deliver that message, and deliver the message multiple times— then about 25 percent of them will come.

Not so pithy, and not so easy. But time spent on the nuances of building a strategy can yield unlikely tactics and partners, which in turn can yield real results. After all, by the end of the Obama administration, 20 million additional people got health insurance. We built it, and with an incredible amount of effort to get them there, they came.

LESSON LEARNED

Using the Persuasion Matrix can help you think about each audience in a thorough and strategic way, opening the way for innovative strategies.

29

Battle with the Bishops

The human services field has no shortage of horror stories. Few, though, are more devastating than those of human-trafficking survivors. Since the federal government is the main source of funding to address human trafficking, survivors of trafficking would come to DC to testify at congressional hearings. They often visited the Administration for Children & Families office and spoke with the people who ran the programs that served them at crucial times. Most of them were trafficked for labor, frequently in the hospitality and agriculture industries, but others were trafficked for sex. For women, the lines between labor and sex trafficking often crossed.

Not surprisingly, women escaping trafficking frequently had to deal with unwanted pregnancies, most commonly the result of coerced sex. But one primary contractor for services to human trafficking victims—the US Conference of Catholic Bishops (USCCB or Bishops)—provided only a limited range of options for pregnant women, excluding birth control and abortion. As Sister Mary Ann Walsh, communication director for the USCCB, said to the *Washington Post* at the time: "The principle of Church teaching is that all sexual encounters be open to life."[1]

Between 2006 and 2011 the Bishops had received more than $19 million to provide services, including housing and counseling, to human trafficking victims. The contract began during the George W. Bush administration, which oversaw a sharp rise in faith-based organizations receiving federal contracts. In 2011 two events coincided: the American Civil Liberties Union (ACLU) sued HHS on the grounds that it was allowing the Catholic Church to impose its beliefs by denying women in federally funded programs reproductive health options, and the Bishops' contract expired.

In the spring of 2011, HHS political appointees carefully crafted a
new Request for Proposals (RFP). An added provision was that there
would be a "strong preference" for applicants offering referrals for family
planning and the full range of gynecological and obstetric care—including abortion. The grantees did not have to provide those services; they
just had to let their clients know that those services were an option and to
provide them with referrals.

Within the Office of Refugee Resettlement (ORR), which administered the human trafficking program, was a small and vocal contingent of
staff more aligned with the Catholic Church than with the Obama administration. As the grantee selection process proceeded to its conclusion, an
independent review team gave the Bishops' proposal higher marks than
those of other applicants. But the requirement for a full range of reproductive health services took them out of the running. HHS had denied
the Bishops the contract, instead splitting the federal funds among three
other organizations: Heartland Human Care Services, Tapestri and the
US Committee for Refugees and Immigrants.

Staff from the Refugee Resettlement office balked. They didn't see the
process as one that led to a decision based on what was legally required.
Instead, they saw sharp-elbowed political appointees interfering with an
objective federal process, and they weren't going to keep quiet about it.

We all need teachers, and Anita Dunn was one of my best. She was strategic *and* tactical and always able to make smart, quick decisions amid
publicly breaking controversies.

It was what I learned from working with Anita that had me, on Halloween night in 2011, in my office at ACF and on the phone with Jerry
Markon of the *Washington Post*. With sources from both the Bishops and
inside HHS, the *Post* was about to portray this change in contractors as
a scandal of political appointee overreach. But Anita taught me that if a
story wasn't going your way, you needed to push back—hard. With the
reporter, and with their editor, if necessary.

I had several calls with Jerry that evening. In between I stayed in contact with communication staff at both HHS and the White House, who
were pushing me to change the frame of the *Post* story. I got Jerry to agree

to include how many dollars had gone to Catholic organizations from HHS (at least $800 million since the mid '90s, including $348 million to the Bishops). This point stood in stark contrast to Sister Mary Ann's statement in a recent blog post that the federal government had an "ABC" policy—Anybody But Catholics.

We also persuaded him to include information about the ACLU suit against HHS. What is legally required should matter here, I argued, not just who got the most points in a review process. And he included a good quote from my boss, Assistant Secretary George Sheldon: "I don't think there was any undue influence exerted to make this grant go one way or another. Ultimately, I felt it was my responsibility to do what I thought was in the best interests of these victims."

In the end, the story was more about long-standing conflicts between the federal government and the Catholic Church than it was about appointee overreach, though that accusation was included. The reporter also noted the history of the Catholic Church challenging Kathleen Sebelius, the secretary of HHS, for her pro-choice positions, at one point advocating that she not be allowed to receive the sacrament of Communion. If we had to have a story about the Catholic Church tangling with the Obama administration, at least we could show the church's intolerance and imperiousness.

Ultimately, it wasn't a story we wanted, but it was a story we could live with.[2] And for me, as a veteran of 12 years of Catholic school, I had to admit to some sense of victory in having engaged in professional battle with the church hierarchy. Sister Mary Ann versus federal official Marrianne. We were well matched.

Several weeks later, I was out at Great Falls, Virginia, with Brendan, who was then 11, and a couple of his friends, hiking on a Sunday morning. This is the same kid who didn't get to go trick or treating on Halloween night because I was working late trying to shape the *Washington Post* story on the Bishops' contract. His dad had to make a choice: stay home and hand out candy or go trick or treating and get candy. Staying home seemed the way to focus on more and younger children.

Driving back into DC from our Sunday morning hike, we got stuck in a traffic jam. I pulled out my Blackberry to check my email. There was a lot of it; the next phase of the Bishops' story had erupted in the Sunday edition of the *Post*. GOP legislators had written to the *Post*, challenging the decision to give the grants to other organizations. The action was framed as anti-Catholic, anti-Christian, and antireligion. It was a coordinated communication assault, with the Bishops fighting—shamelessly and ironically—for federal funds to serve victims of sex crimes.

The traffic started moving and I handed my Blackberry to Brendan, who diligently started reading emails and *Washington Post* letters to me as I drove. We were no longer going home but going to my office where I could get my computer and some documents to start working on drafting a general strategy and specific responses. After we got downtown and went through security, the boys sat quietly at the conference table in my office while I shot off a few emails, made some calls, and gathered my things. They were unusually subdued, probably taken aback by my intensity in the moment, not to mention the spacious office with a large picture of Barack Obama looming over the conference table and a large American flag standing in the corner.

Over the coming months, the controversy continued, with volleys back and forth in national publications and on Capitol Hill. The House Committee on Oversight and Government Reform, chaired by Darrell Issa (R-CA), sponsored a hearing where they grilled ACF officials and gave grandstanding speeches slamming the Obama administration for waging war against the Catholic Church. Two other points of contention—the HHS rule that private insurers must cover contraceptives and support for gay marriage—were never far from the surface as further evidence of the administration's hostility to conservative religious values.

In March 2012 the resolution of the legal case brought by the ACLU helped close this chapter. Judge Richard G. Stearns ruled in favor of the ACLU. His decision read, in part: "No one is arguing that the USCCB can be mandated by government to provide abortion or contraceptive services or be discriminated against for its refusal to do so. Rather, this case is about the limits of the government's ability to delegate to a religious institution the right to use taxpayer money to impose its beliefs on others (who may or may not share them)."[3]

In the end, because the Catholic Bishops were denied this contract, some women who had been victims of labor and sex trafficking got back some control over their lives. They could decide whether they would have a child. And they could decide whom they wanted to be the father of their children.

That's not the type of victory that gets a lot of attention in an electoral cycle. It affects a small number of less-powerful people. But it is the type of policy that honors the humanity and agency of each person served by federal programs. And it's the type of policy that took an enormous amount of effort to fight for, and win, during the Obama administration.

LESSON LEARNED

When working with the media, particularly singularly powerful outlets, sometimes you have to fight for the story you want—with the reporter, with the editor, and on deadline.

30

Unaccompanied in San Antonio

The cinderblock room was large and windowless. Long folding tables formed a U-shape around three sides. At each of more than a dozen of these tables, a social worker was setting up a computer, arranging piles of files. Some had bowls of candy. They were preparing for a day of direct client service to migrant children who entered the country unaccompanied by adults.

It was a new use for this space. We were at Lackland Joint Air Force Base outside of San Antonio, a sprawling base that was a heavily guarded city unto itself. It was summer 2014, and the US Department of Defense (DOD) had once again been called into duty to allow HHS to use its facilities to house unaccompanied children coming over the southern border. By July, we had 1,000 children there.

I was sitting with other staff on folding chairs at the center of that large room when the double metal doors opened and a staff person came in with two teenage girls. One looked wide-eyed and stunned, and the other burst into tears as soon as she entered the room and looked around.

"Every time someone goes and gets a kid and tells them it's time for an appointment, they think they are about to be deported," explained one of the staff I was sitting with.

Fear and anxiety were relentless for these kids. They had traveled thousands of miles to get here. A few were lucky—they had enough money to ensure their safe passage to and across the Rio Grande and had arrived in fairly good physical and psychological condition. But most endured unfathomable suffering and trauma on their long journeys, constantly dodging authorities until they entered the United States, at which point they would surrender themselves to the Border Patrol. Typically, they would spend a day or two in a border detention facility and then be transferred to HHS shelters. Everything felt uncertain and threatening to them. They still feared that at any moment they could be sent back to Central America, undoing sometimes years of planning and months of risk and suffering to escape unbearable, often life-threatening, conditions.

This HHS program had labored in obscurity for years, so much so that it retained an impolitic name: the Unaccompanied Alien Children (UAC) program. In the warren of the federal government it was housed in the Office of Refugee Resettlement, in the Administration for Children & Families, in the US Department of Health and Human Services.

In a typical year 7,000 or so minors entered the United States without a parent or legal guardian. They mostly came across the southern border but some came in on ships from other continents. The UAC program was charged with providing them with housing, health care, clothing, food, education, and other services, while social workers matched the children and teens with family members or friends who could take custody of them. A small percentage ended up in foster care.

The last year of Barack Obama's first term, 2012, was not a typical one. That spring the monthly population of unaccompanied children coming over the border tripled. We were desperate for new beds, while public protests greeted every attempt to open new shelters. When we looked at shuttered colleges or hospitals, for example, we were met with protest at the idea that any town would become an asylum for "illegal aliens," even if they were children. As the number of youth coming over the border escalated and rumors spread about where they were going, protestors even lay down in front of school buses that turned out to be full of local children. With thousands of kids on our hands, there was no time to do a gradual persuasion process, wooing communities to shelter these kids. Nor was there time for major building renovations. Hundreds of beds were required immediately.

Melissa Jacks, then the chief of staff at the Administration for Children & Families, created a detailed spreadsheet of all the possible places where we could add beds, mostly through existing federal contractors expanding their services. Given the rate of intake and out-placements, we knew we needed at least 800 more beds.

The DOD had numerous mothballed facilities in secure locations. Given the history of gangs following some of these youth out of Central America, the secure part was important. (In one particularly gruesome incident, a gang leader based in El Salvador learned the address of a Florida shelter and shipped a package with severed fingers to a teenage boy there.)

While we were hunting for permanent placements, we got a call from the *New York Times* about the controversial temporary facilities. The reporter, Manny Fernandez, said other people he interviewed had told him we weren't taking enough care to ensure safe placements where the kids would receive all the services and rights outlined by law.

Melissa and I had been looking through the spreadsheet in my office when Manny called. I put him on hold while we did some quick math about how many more beds we could add with all the locations we had secured. It added up to 851 permanent beds that we could safely say we would be able to bring on. I picked the phone back up and said: "We have 851 permanent, licensed beds coming online between now and June." Further, I said, we would shut down all temporary facilities over the summer. We were betting on a repeat of a similar pattern in all previous years: that the flow of unaccompanied children peaked in the spring and slowed considerably in the summer.

Those comments were not cleared in advance when I talked to the reporter. And during the Obama administration, every utterance was cleared—far too often by people not qualified to make the judgment call. But sometimes effective media relations require you to go out on a limb. In this case, I felt compelled to deliver a clear message of "we got this." Those with appointments in presidential administrations are not observers of events. We are shapers of events. That has to be conveyed, always. Anything less can undermine public confidence.

The story was posted just a few hours after we talked.[4] Without my quote saying what we were planning to do, the piece would have only been criticism of the administration's handling of the crisis. The *New York Times* pushed us to declare a detailed solution—851 new licensed beds—and by doing so we committed the agency to making it happen. The media, in this case, genuinely acted as "the fourth estate."

⊠

The push factors for immigration—violence and poverty in Central America—had increased exponentially in just two years, leading to new record numbers of unaccompanied youth coming over the border in 2014. Once again, we needed to call on the Department of Defense.

We all learned a lot working together in 2012. Military public affairs is well staffed and capable. At our very first meeting, DOD public affairs staff bristled at the term *alien* in the program's name. We immediately shed the name, which we used because it was in the legislation authorizing the program, and just called it the Unaccompanied Children program. (The DOD is not where one would expect guidance on cultural sensitivity in language, but there it was.) In 2012 the discomfort that the DOD had about playing this sheltering role was so profound that on one early conference call there were no fewer than four generals on the line. They challenged, they discussed, and they let their feelings be known, but at the end of the day there was one question: what is the mission? Once that mission was decided and clear, the discussion was over and everyone got to work. It was an aspect of military culture that I appreciated immensely.

When we returned to the DOD in 2014, though, they had learned enough from 2012 that they wanted to refine their rules of engagement. There was no way they were going to fight the last war. This time, they insisted on a Memorandum of Understanding (MOU). One of their many conditions in this MOU was that an HHS communication person be on site at all times to manage the external affairs and media relations demands. My staff and I, and a few other communication staff from other HHS agencies, took turns doing one-to-two-week rotations in San Antonio.

Our communications office learned a few things from 2012, too. The Office of Refugee Resettlement had always been strict about security and privacy at their facilities. "The children aren't animals in a zoo," they would say, supporting their bans of any media at shelters. But this approach worked against building trust and confidence in the services we were providing. We also had the added communication burden of public confusion between the US Border Patrol facilities and the HHS shelters. At the former, fences were erected in large, overly air-conditioned warehouse-like buildings, while people sat around wrapped in foil-like blankets. Our facilities, however, were nothing like that. They were institutional, yes, but comfortable, with good food, classes, health care, recreational activities, and many caring and dedicated staff. The blankets were made of cotton; the air temperature was comfortable.

We talked ORR into some compromises. First, when the shelter was set up and before the kids were placed there, we allowed journalists to tour the facility at Lackland Air Force Base. They saw the bunk rooms, the medical clinic, the dining area, the classrooms, the recreation areas. They were walked through the intake procedures and how a typical day went for a young person (ages 12 to 17).

While they were not permitted to bring cameras or to tape or film, we took a broad range of quality still shots and gave them all access. After the kids came, we shot B-roll and took more still shots, ensuring that no kids were identifiable, and made all of that available to the media. The still shots also included art produced by the kids that they hung around their beds, often reflecting scenes from their home countries.

The media used every bit of what we provided and were very appreciative. They had collateral for their news reports, and we were able to deliver a clear visual message about the quality of conditions at the shelter.

Another big change between 2012 and 2014 was working with the Federal Emergency Management Administration (FEMA). It had set up a Joint Information Center (JIC) to coordinate activities between HHS, the DOD, FEMA, the White House, and any other federal agency or staff who might touch the immigration emergency. By mid-May 2014 I was working part of the time out of my ACF office and part of the time out of FEMA—roughly six hours at each location, every day. We had standing check-in cross-agency conference calls seven days a week.

FEMA staff who commanded the effort had the authority to demand immediate decisions from anyone. After years of passive resistance from the White House and HHS that I had no power to counter, it was a pleasure to be in the room with someone with the authority to compel action. "What do you mean the White House hasn't responded yet?" I remember a FEMA commander asking after just an hour after the White House had been contacted. He immediately moved up the White House chain and got the clearance we needed to move forward with a decision.

FEMA had an open-concept office designed for a primarily remote staff. There were only a handful of permanent offices; most employees brought their computers and set up in any open workspace. One large room had long, high-top tables at one end, with pods of four low-walled cubicles across the rest of the floor and "huddle rooms" along the inside wall where you could have phone calls and small meetings. The JIC was located in a separate room lined with large-screen TVs. The unaccompanied-minor team tended to work together at the large table just outside the JIC.

The DOD wasn't the only agency committed to not fighting the last war. FEMA's communication shop had learned a lot from Hurricane Katrina in 2005. FEMA personnel watched as members of the Coast Guard were hailed as heroes, while FEMA was portrayed as bumbling and mired in red tape. Both agencies had clear missions and dedicated staff, but they had very different communication practices. Specifically: everyone who was in the Coast Guard was authorized to talk to the media at any time. Their only caveat is that they could only talk about their own job—nothing about policies, politics, or agency-wide decisions. What was their responsibility? Were they having trouble attaining or transporting materials they needed? Were they getting an assist from local residents? How many hours had they worked that day? If it was within the context of their assigned duties, they could talk about it. This meant journalists not only got good color for their stories but they also came to respect the individual Coast Guard staff, and that came through in their stories.

FEMA staff, meanwhile, lived with restrictions more common in the federal government—that only a few people were ever authorized to talk to the media and even they could only use cleared talking points. From my experience, this was at its most extreme in HHS. When I worked with the US Department of Education or Housing and Urban Development, their communications staff were able to regularly interact with the media without excessive approval from above. The DOD and Department of Labor communicators also had more flexibility. After Katrina, FEMA changed its policy, authorizing all staff to talk to the media at any time about their own jobs. Media training for all staff became a routine part of orientation and continued professional development. Imagine what it could do for the federal government's image if this was an across-the-board practice.

In San Antonio in the summer of 2014, when I was on assignment at
Lackland Joint Air Force Base, I was invited to attend a community meeting called by Presbyterian Disaster Assistance and the San Antonio Area
Voluntary Organizations Active in Disaster (VOAD). It was held at the
First Presbyterian Church downtown, where about 125 people were sitting on folding chairs in a large meeting room. Tables were set up across
the front with a podium, where the moderator and the speakers were,
with refreshments in the back. I sat down in one of the back rows, hoping
to be inconspicuous.

Speakers leaned hard into Christian charity and the responsibility
to care for children, and when the floor opened up for questions or comments the first several speakers were similarly compassionate, saying
what churches they represented and asking how they could help.

"We're happy to welcome an official from the Obama administration," the moderator said during the comment section. So much for being
inconspicuous. "These children have been through a lot and are targeted
for violence," the local paper quoted me as saying. "We thank you for everything you're doing. You represent the majority."[5]

I was stunned at the consistent, positive tone of the community meeting. When I complemented the meeting organizers afterward, I learned
that they were intentional in their approach. Not only did they have speakers emphasizing the most sympathetic details of the children's plights
but they also knew exactly who was going to speak first in the open-mic
session, understanding that the first speakers always set the tone. Their
framing of caring for children as Christian duty was both genuine and
brilliant messaging for this churchy Texas audience.

Back at Lackland Air Force Base, in the cinderblock room, young people
gathered one at a time or in small groups at each table while others waited
their turn. It was the social worker's job to help young people identify an
eligible family member or friend in the United States who could come
and get them, taking them into their custody while the youth awaited
an asylum hearing. Young people pored over Facebook pages with social

workers, looking for their people. Some were ready with names and phone numbers right away.

One by one, connections were made. Periodically, a joyfully loud interaction would punctuate the typically somber room. A child found an *abuela*; a parent found their child. And they would soon be on their way to pick the child up. The youth would leave with anticipated court dates. They weren't legal yet, but they were safe. And, they hoped, on their way to a new life.

LESSON LEARNED

Communications staff need to be able to lead. At times, decisions have to be made in the moment, without permission, to ensure a positive and accurate public image for a program or an organization.

31

Thorny Human Resource

Some names, locations, and details in the following story have been changed to protect the privacy of the employees involved.

Starting in early 2014, the first thing that came up when I googled my name were blog posts accusing me of protecting child sex abusers on Spirit Lake Reservation in North Dakota. This was more than two years before a lone gunman entered Comet Pizza in Washington, DC, intending to break up a rumored child sex ring, allegedly run by left-wingers out of the pizzeria's basement.

The child sex ring didn't exist. The basement didn't even exist. But with that December 2016 event—in the last full month of the Obama administration—news about QAnon and right-wing conspiracy theories related to child sex abuse began to spread widely.

We knew nothing about any of that in 2014. The accusations focused on me started in an anonymous blog called "Restless Spirit" that attacked my then-boss, Assistant Secretary George Sheldon, for stopping "the reports of children being raped, abused, and worse" at Spirit Lake. For some reason, the blogger thought I was Sheldon's boss, referring to him as one of my "hangar of flying monkeys."[6]

"Heads Up Marrianne" was the title of one blog post; "Watch your Queen" was the subhead. "McMullen was not misled by [Sheldon]," the anonymous blogger wrote. "Nor was he betraying her trust in how he performed his job while under her supervision. He was in fact, carrying out her directives, with her full and complete knowledge, and at her pleasure."[7]

How did I get in these peculiar crosshairs? In 2013 Sheldon promoted me from the director of public affairs to deputy assistant secretary for external affairs, putting communications, the Freedom of Information

Act office, and all 10 regional offices and their staffs under my direction. I went from supervising a 5-person communications shop to managing more than 120 staff in 11 offices across the country. The Office of Regional Operations was notoriously dysfunctional. Regional administrators had their own separate fiefdoms, each acting independently and with little direction or accountability. Regional staff sizes varied wildly, and no two offices were doing the same work.

These were a few of my conclusions after spending the early fall of 2013 visiting all 10 regional offices and interviewing every staff person and other key local stakeholders. People were stunningly straightforward. One staff person, when I asked her what she did, responded: "Not much." (I later found out that she was in constant conflict with her supervisor, and she thought her lack of productivity would reflect poorly on him.)

I wrote up a detailed and critical report on the "state of the regions," with recommendations that would take the rest of Obama's term to implement. This approach, and this report, made me few friends. Multiple retirements took place in the months following the report, allowing me to start slowly bringing on capable staff committed to the agency's mission. But several regional administrators and their staffs tenaciously resisted the increased demands and accountability, leading to years of challenge and drama.

In January 2014, the same month that I released the State of the Regions Report, Spirit Lake chairman Russ MacDonald came to DC to meet with administration officials. He met with me and Lillian Sparks, the director of the Administration for Native Americans, to talk specifically about one of my regional staff: Robert Murphy, a regional administrator based in Omaha, Nebraska. It was understood that Murphy had been the source of information for the anonymous blogger and other right-wing outlets about alleged sex abuse at Spirit Lake. Our email exchanges and his summaries of our meetings and phone calls popped up in right-wing blogs and other outlets, who saw him as a whistleblower. In his versions, I was held up as someone who was obstructing investigations of child abuse in Indian Country.

"How can someone talk about their boss that way, publicly, and still keep their job?" Chairman MacDonald asked us at that DC meeting. Good question. Embarrassing question.

The chairman wanted to talk about how much trouble Murphy's inflammatory accusations were causing on the reservation. MacDonald had invited Murphy to come to Spirit Lake to lead an independent investigation and provide recommendations on how to address abuse if it was substantiated. Murphy wasn't about to take him up on that.

Murphy's history in the federal government dated back to the Nixon administration. By the time I met him he was not carrying out any of the functions of a federal employee, considering himself, first and foremost, a whistleblower about child sex abuse, particularly on Native American reservations. He wrote long and detailed "reports" that included dozens of pages of meandering single-spaced text with salacious details about child abuse, accusing the Administration for Children & Families of being complicit in all of it. He never even pretended to do the work required of a regional administrator. He provided no direction to staff, was frequently absent, and was there for minimal hours whenever he did come to the office.

Firing him for cause—for not doing any recognizable job whatsoever—should have been easy. But it wasn't. I was advised to proceed as if he had whistleblower protection, which meant I was not to discipline him for anything related to Spirit Lake or his communication about Tribal children being at risk. That turned out to not be a problem. First, though, it was important to look into what was actually happening at Spirit Lake.

When we arrived at the Spirit Lake Tribal offices, a television camera man was filming as three of us from ACF walked into a small conference room. I was with JooYuen Chang, director of ACF's Children's Bureau, and Lillian Sparks Robinson, director of the Administration for Native Americans. Our first meeting during our three-day visit was with the most vocal critics of ACF, including those who were publicly accusing ACF of concealing child sex abuse. I told the cameraman that this was not a public meeting but that he was welcome to call me any time during our visit. I gave him my card, and he left.

It was an odd meeting. We had many questions for this group of advocates about specific incidents, but instead of responding with details they kept aggressively challenging us with broad questions like "Who is responsible for the safety of the children at Spirit Lake?" (Um, I don't know, maybe the adults at Spirit Lake?)

After our meeting, we visited the office in that same building where the child welfare cases were filed. Stacks and stacks of files and overflowing file cabinets lined the room. And they weren't organized by name; they were organized by the date of incidents. It was a mess. How could a caseworker even track related incidents to a new report of child abuse or neglect?

The next morning, as we had breakfast at our hotel, the large-screen TV in the common dining area was showing news coverage of our visit. There we were, entering the conference room with surprised glances at the cameraman. "There's our girls," said the woman maintaining the breakfast buffet. The hotel staff had clearly adopted their "celebrity" visitors. We also learned from news coverage that the advocates we had met with had secretly recorded our entire visit and posted the audio on a website. That explained their performative challenges. But our federal-official fact-finding approach didn't make for very dramatic content.

In our few days in North Dakota, it felt like we met with half the population of the reservation and the adjacent county. We met with school, health, and county officials, Tribal leaders, and Tribal leadership critics. I had more than 50 pages of detailed, typed notes by the time we left. Months of follow-up ensued. JooYuen developed and presented a range of recommendations from the Children's Bureau and mobilized some foundation contacts to help the Tribe install and start using a digitized case tracking system. Lillian testified at a congressional hearing about Spirit Lake Child Welfare, and we all met with top officials at the Bureau of Indian Affairs, the only federal agency that really had any jurisdiction to do anything more than make recommendations.

But Robert Murphy was still a regional administrator. His disruptive presence was brought up in more than a few of our meetings at Spirit Lake. And it seemed that our focus on addressing problems at Spirit Lake didn't mollify him. It actually seemed to provoke him.

In August 2014, four months after our Spirit Lake visit, Murphy sent a letter to then HHS assistant secretary Mark Greenberg, notifying him that "4 Native American thugs" had broken into the home of "one of his sources" on the Spirit Lake Reservation.

"Because of your refusal to allow any of us who wish to move the children of Sprit Lake into safe placements . . . Because of your refusal to control the efforts of your allies in ACF, BIA, DOJ and the state and tribe to intimidate us into silence, you had a direct hand in that attempted break-in yesterday. . . . If those thugs had not fled when they did, there would have been significant blood shed on that farm yesterday. It would have been theirs."

The comment about blood spilling gave us cause to pass this on to the federal police, who then questioned Murphy. It also allowed me to issue a formal reprimand regarding the accusatory and threatening tone of his letter.

Months later, in early 2015, I visited the Omaha office. Bob Murphy was nowhere to be found. I learned that he had planned to be on medical leave for six weeks but had never requested leave or notified anyone that he would be gone. If he had requested leave, it would have been granted. But he felt no need to be accountable in any way because he hadn't been for years. The only thing he did in return for his handsome GS-15-level paycheck was cause mayhem. I wrote up Murphy for being AWOL, a violation that called for a 14-day suspension, and immediately named an interim regional administrator. Simultaneously, he was seeking protection as a whistleblower with the Office of Special Counsel, while I kept building up a record of personnel infractions not related to his alleged whistleblowing.

This was an incredibly lonely struggle. My political appointee colleagues, focused on developing and implementing new policy, were not interested in the laborious procedures required to remove low-performing staff. And legal and labor relations offices, who should have been providing direction to me, were minimally responsive. Other regional administrators were also bucking my efforts to reform the office and increase accountability.

One day, as I was looking through my files to create a timeline for the incoming new director of the Office of Regional Operations, Mishaela Durán, I was overwhelmed by the amount of conflict I was reviewing. "I just burst into tears in my office," I wrote in my journal. "I feel so alone and so relentlessly under attack. I am so worn out. So ready to go."

But there was still more than a year left in the Obama administration, and the White House Office of Personnel was urging all political appointees who could stay until the end to do so. And we could see progress. Going into 2016, 6 of the 10 regional administrators had retired after I required work plans in accordance with administration priorities and accountability for achievement.

In the spring of 2016, Murphy racked up another significant infraction. This, from everything I understood about personnel management in a federal environment, created a long-enough list of disciplinary actions to issue a termination notice. And Mishaela, now his direct supervisor, had more than enough moxie to take on this fight. When we issued a personnel action for termination, Murphy hired a flamboyantly aggressive attorney who conducted himself like a man who had watched too many legal dramas on TV. He accused me of attacking Murphy because he was a white man and threatened to sue me and ACF for discrimination. The Office of Special Counsel had recently turned down Murphy's whistleblower case, so the whistleblower defense never came up in the attorney's passionate soliloquy delivered in an incongruously modest, windowless meeting room at HHS.

Murphy appealed his termination, and I spent hours on a response to his appeal, bringing in many details about years of performance and conduct issues. HHS' lawyers advised against this broad approach, but if this appeal were to go before a judge, I wanted the judge to have the full story. And I wanted the full story to be on the record and in Murphy's personnel file. On Friday, May 6, in the face of Murphy's aggressive legal counsel, the HHS Office of General Counsel recommended I issue a third suspension rather than terminate.

I was incredulous. I wrote a final memo upholding the termination, effective immediately. I sent it to his attorney and to our counsel. Murphy's attorney called me in a panic.

"There's no effective date," he said.

"It says effective immediately," I said.

"Do you mean this very moment or at the close of business?"

"This moment is good," I said.

I didn't realize how unconventional and unpredictable my action was until I watched the attorney's complete discombobulation. Perhaps it was his predictably routine negotiations with HHS attorneys, and his experience with passive political appointees, but he never thought I was going to uphold the termination against the advice of counsel. Even after everything Murphy had done to disparage me and embarrass our agency.

By the following Monday, May 9, Murphy had submitted retirement papers dated Thursday, May 5, the day prior to the official termination. He was protecting his retirement. I didn't care; I just wanted him gone. I signed his retirement papers.

It was finally over. It took three years.

On June 7 I was back in Omaha when Hillary Clinton won the California primary overwhelmingly, putting her over the threshold of becoming the first woman nominated by a major party for a president. I was stopping in the city on my way to speak at the National Energy and Utility Affordability Conference about my work partnering with utility companies to do outreach about the Affordable Care Act.

I was there to clean out Murphy's office. In crime dramas, there's frequently a moment when investigators enter the home of the perpetrator and find a secret room with the clippings and photos plastered all over the walls that reveal the perp's obsession. That was Murphy's office, though less visually dramatic. The windowless room in the center of the floor was lined with two-foot-high stacks of paper. News clippings about child sex abuse dominated the piles, along with printouts of emails and letters attacking ACF and Obama administration leadership.

I didn't find a single work product—no project plans, no draft goal statements, no indication of direction to staff or responses to management requests, no personnel reviews. It was all sex abuse and management battles. With each passing hour, rifling through and inventorying all the contents of his office, I had a fresh sense of outrage that this extremely disturbed person had been holding down a high-level federal position for so many years.

By the end of that year, and the end of the Obama administration, 8 of the 10 regional administrators had been replaced, regional staff sizes had been reduced, and every staff team was accountable for moving work forward on the administration's highest priorities. Mishaela Durán had become a powerhouse director of the Office of Regional Operations and was moving all reforms forward with tenacity, work she was to continue through the Trump administration.

Though eight years have passed since these episodes, if you scroll down far enough through Google entries under my name, you will still find my association with protecting child sex abusers at Spirit Lake Reservation. I can't imagine any management-training program that could prepare you for paying that particular price for a workplace performance improvement effort.

LESSON LEARNED

One of the hardest responsibilities of a supervisor is to address problem employees. But it is critical to do so—for the sake of the mission, the organization, and your other employees.

32

Internal Communications Matters

In 2011, when I came to the Administration for Children & Families, one of the largest divisions of HHS, the communication challenge was overwhelming. There was no branding for the agency—no shared messaging, no logo, no colors—just a loose collection of websites from each of the major program offices, each with their own look and each with pretty much the original design (or lack thereof) from when government websites were first emerging in the aughts.

Given the priority of establishing branding and building an entirely new public-facing presence, it was four years before I could focus on internal communication. With 12 offices across the country and 1,200 staff, internal communication was a serious and important endeavor.

Internal communication is how an organization conveys information to its own staff: newsletters, intranet, emails from the boss, staff meetings, shared digital platforms, bulletin boards, special events. Frequently, the communications staff play a supporting role in this function, providing technical skills to the executive and human resources offices. Often, though, we play a leadership role. Not that we generally want to, mind you. Staff dedicated to internal communication is a rarity, particularly in the nonprofit and government sectors. Internal communication can feel like an extra, unwelcome distraction from what seems a more important and visible public audience. Smart organizational leaders, though, know that internal communication is critical to an effective organization.

We established the Internal Communication Task Force, which was charged with identifying internal communication systems that would have a positive impact on employee productivity and morale. The task force had 18 members from across the agency, with additional staff consulted as specific work groups carried out their work. Members were chosen for their considerable experience across ACF's program and staff offices and were identified as people with the drive and experience to effect positive cultural change. They shared a vision of a stronger, more productive agency.

The task force initially convened in the summer of 2015, and numerous work groups formed over the next few months to develop specific categories of recommendations. These work groups focused on evaluation, the intranet, all-staff meetings and events, internal email best practices, departmental communication best practices, and communicating within the headquarters building.

Over 18 months, each work group produced specific products and recommendations, from a list of internal communication channels, to a tip sheet on email best practices. This approach to improvement allowed for organization-wide investment in and awareness of internal communications' importance. The broad investment in staff hours meant a greater likelihood that the recommended practices would be carried out.

Whole books have been written, and rightly so, about effective internal communication. But here are the most useful tips that this team developed and how they can be applied at any organization.

EVALUATION

Determine a way to measure your progress. This could include intranet site traffic and open and click-through rates on newsletters. If your organization conducts a regular employee survey to measure morale, make sure internal communication questions are included, such as satisfaction levels with availability of information and with communication from management. If you don't do a general survey, consider doing a short, communication-specific survey. Know what your baseline is and set goals for improvement. Set a regular schedule for checking on your progress.

INTRANET

Information for staff has to be self-service—to be available to employees when *they* want it, not just when the boss decides to share it. A well-organized intranet with a strong search engine is the backbone of staff communication. Rule one for your intranet: keep it current. One visit that leads an employee to dated information or a section that hasn't been updated in a year will undermine the intranet as a reliable source of information. Maintain a minimum schedule of weekly updates. Ruthlessly excise old content.

Depending on the size of your organization, consider a formal structure for intranet governance. For small- or midsized organizations, this could be one editorial board that represents different parts of the organization. For a large organization, it could be three teams: a governance team of decision makers, a content team, and a technical support team to ensure strong functionality.

When new employees start, make sure IT sets up their computers to default to the intranet landing page when they open their web browsers. Provide clear instructions to all staff on how to set the intranet as their default page and encourage them to do so.

MEETINGS

Nothing sucks the life out of a workday like a bad meeting. And very few hours can be more stimulating at work than a good one. So get this right.

Agendas need to be planned thoughtfully and well in advance. This agenda, and any materials that need to be shared, should be available to all participants several days ahead and attached to the meeting invitation. During meetings, track decisions and follow-up tasks in a central location. Do a follow-up email that lists next steps and points people to where materials are stored.

For large meetings—like all-staff meetings—periodically do quick, three-to-five question surveys circulated digitally right after the meeting to get a feel for what you are doing that is going over well with staff, and what isn't. If you want to dig deeper, do some staff focus groups with key opinion leaders. If you can be in the same room when you do this, provide lunch.

As many businesses have moved into permanent remote status following the COVID-19 pandemic, some web-based meetings have turned more into work sessions. The meeting space becomes a time when everyone is working together as if in the same open office. The team can be discussing a project and realize that a specific task needs to be done—email someone to check on the progress of a task, for example. Since everyone is sitting at their computers, one person can go ahead and do that, while others continue on with another conversation. Often, before the meeting is even completed, you will hear back from the person you emailed and the whole team can be updated on the progress. Progress has happened as a result of and during the meeting. Whereas in "before times" you would have written yourself a note and followed up after the meeting, the perpetually connected nature of working and meeting online allows for work and meetings to flow more seamlessly. This is a good development and one that we still need to learn to use more effectively.

EMAILS

Say you've spent an hour in a poorly planned and poorly run meeting, only to face 20 new emails that came in while you were in that meeting. Double ugh. Everyone benefits if we don't email unnecessarily and that when we do so, we do it well.

Consider the subject line. It's not the "subjects" line. Keep every email to one subject and make that clear in the subject line. No email is more likely to go unanswered, and to overwhelm its recipient, than one that covers a half-dozen different points and raises as many questions. If the topic is that nuanced or confidential, you need a discussion, not an email.

Timing matters. The research on when exactly the most emails get opened and responded to has shifted over the years, but in general Tuesday, Wednesday, and Thursday mornings are best. Friday afternoons are the worst. Emailing outside of working hours—such as before 8 a.m., after 5 p.m., or on weekends—is not only ineffective in terms of open and response rates but it also has an additional morale-damaging effect of signaling that you expect people to be working at all hours. Stop it.

Also: it's important to remember that your inbox is full of other people's priorities. Now, your job may be exactly that—to address other people's priorities. But for most professionals, if you are going to be successful, you have your own goals that you need to prioritize. Don't be the bad workplace citizen who doesn't respond to messages, but do be the employee who values her priorities enough to stay focused on them and to prioritize them over others' immediate needs.

SHARED DIGITAL PLATFORMS

A shared digital space to store and communicate about work has become indispensable. Microsoft Teams, Microsoft SharePoint, Basecamp, Slack—the platforms are endless. These allow teams to store their work products, develop and update work plans, maintain calendars, track hours and budgets—all in one place. Most important for communications, it allows for one version of documents in progress, rather than emailing around versions and never being quite sure who has the current version or if the version you are working on has everyone's changes. Awesome progress.

But if they aren't done well, shared workspaces can also be a source of frustration. They can start looking like a digital version of a kitchen junk drawer—lots of unrelated items scattered about, making any one thing difficult to find. Shared workspaces need to start with a clear operational goal: "why do we have this site?" or "what is its function?" From there a file structure should be developed, with the most important information on the home or landing page. This may be a calendar, for example, or a Gannt chart of a workplan. It's also good to establish naming conventions for files. Keep the site current, and be consistent in using it for all work related to that project.

Like any communication, internal communication is part art, part science. It's a management skill, aided by technical communication skills. The art comes in determining what should be a text, what should be an email, what should be a meeting agenda item, what should be a phone call. One of the jobs of a manager is setting these parameters for your team so that staff aren't bothered by too much of any one of these communication methods. (We all have our favorites.)

The point of all internal communications is to get your staff team moving steadily and effectively in the right direction to achieve the organization's goals. To that end, those goals have to be a central part of the message in all communication. Those responsible for crafting communication should have the primary strategic goals, the vision, the mission of the organization in front of them at all times so that they are incorporating those into internal messaging—preferably in a way that feels organic, not forced. (More art, that.)

Finally, while many are messengers in internal communication, it's important that the principal—your CEO or the equivalent—be a consistent and primary messenger. "Cascading" communication is when one level of the organization communicates to the next, which is then responsible for communicating to the next level down. This is a weak communication practice. There is too much room for the communication to stop and for the messages to change. Principal leaders have to communicate with all staff directly. This can be in all-staff meetings and emails, participation in team meetings, wandering around the office, quality time during staff retreats, or preferably all of the above. Leaders need to do these things repeatedly and reliably, staying mindful of the key goals of the organization and the role each staff person plays in fulfilling those goals.

Your organization's external brand will be aided by strong internal communications that get everyone focused on the same goals.

LESSON LEARNED

Engage staff to establish a solid infrastructure of channels and practices to achieve organization-wide strong internal communication. It will ultimately build your culture and serve your mission.

33

Management Masters

How on earth could anyone ever be prepared for this job? I probably asked myself that question every day for my first 10 months in the Obama administration.

I tried to imagine a management experience that would have provided adequate preparation. A senior spot in a large, complex organization with staff and offices all over the country? A powerful, highly visible CEO to report up to and a large team to oversee? Maybe. But people with those jobs would have never taken the salary cut to come into the federal government. Nor would they have been likely to comply with federal conflict-of-interest rules that would have required them to sell most of their stock.

The fact is that most political appointees who take up their positions are not, perhaps cannot, be prepared for what the job will require of them. It's no wonder that the typical appointee lasts less than two years; it's hard to withstand being that overwhelmed day after day. The daily stress of facing more work than you could ever possibly accomplish can be unbearable, particularly for high achievers who are used to being on top of their game.

I was 10 months in when I had an epiphany: I had learned which person to call for an answer to any question that came up in my agency. I had gained an understanding of more than a dozen major offices and the 70+ distinct programs that they ran. I certainly couldn't answer all questions, but it was an enormous accomplishment just to know whom to ask what. I was starting to internalize the agency. After *10 months* on the job.

The advantage of managing in a federal environment, though, was the number of incredibly competent people to learn from. I was surrounded by high achievers. Many of them came from a level of privilege that was jarring; their smooth, short paths to success had nothing but on-ramps. Still, they were crazy smart and they had chosen to deploy their advantages for good.

Penny Pritzker, who began serving as Obama's secretary of commerce in June 2013, was a prominent example. The Pritzker family, of the Hyatt hotel fortune, has been on Forbes's list of top 10 wealthiest families since Forbes started making that list in 1982. Penny Pritzker had to sell her interest in a whopping 221 companies and resign from 158 entities, including the Hyatt Board of Directors, to join the Obama administration.[8]

In March of 2014 Pritzker was at a Women's History Month event at the White House with Sylvia Burwell, then-director of the White House Office of Management and Budget who later became Secretary of HHS, and Sally Jewell, secretary of the interior and former CEO of REI. I was among the 50 or so senior women appointees who were invited to a discussion with them. They were sharing their top tips for professional success.

"There are a few things I've noticed coming from the private sector to public," Pritzker said. "First, running a meeting well is important. It's something that people don't seem to know how to do. So many meetings are held without a good structure. It needs to be clear what you are going to do in the meeting—there has to be a clear reason why everyone is in the room, and then we have to be clear what we are going to do when we leave the meeting."

It's a prosaic tip. But it's the one I most remember from that day and that I frequently quote to others. It's a point that is fundamental to everything from productivity to morale. Bad, ineffective, aimless meetings just suck the life out a workday, and out of your staff.

Pritzker's points about the importance of teams also resonated with me. "The most valuable asset you will ever have is the people on your team," she said. Good managers know that the key to their success is not what they can produce independently but what they can inspire and facilitate from a larger group of people. Management is taking the power of human productivity and deploying it at scale. And if a manager can create a strong, unified culture in her team, there's a synergistic effect that spurs even greater productivity because people want to perform for and with each other.

It was good to be reminded of this at this moment, in this room on the White House grounds, but I learned this lesson first at my Dad's service station. The only management approach he brought was from his experience in a large, extended family. It was an approach that combined interdependence, accountability, and personal connection, even affection. This became one of many moments when I thought about the impact of class in our country. I couldn't help but wonder had I been born into the Pritzker family and she into the McMullen family, would I be the one saying that from the stage?

"It's important to take risks—calculated risks. You have to be willing to put yourself in the line of fire," Pritzker said in closing, surprising me. I have repeatedly taken risks that have put my livelihood on the line. Sometimes I suffered for it in the short term, but the risks all paid off in the long term. It was difficult to imagine how a Pritzker could ever be at risk, but clearly individual perceptions of risk are multifaceted.

Sally Jewell also came to the administration from the private sector. She started as an oil engineer, then went into banking, after which her interest in the outdoors took her into REI. I'm sure becoming secretary of the interior wasn't on her career trajectory, but you could see how it could be her dream job.

The tips she shared with other women leaders that day were more global, less tactical.

She named three trends that all leaders will have to deal with. One: working in a time of constrained resources. Two: managing a generational transformation as the baby boomers retire, millennials start assuming leadership, and Gen Z enters the workforce. And three: climate change. In the coming years, all leadership will take place within those three contexts, Jewell said. So far, her forecast is holding up.

The leader many of us were most curious about, though, was Sylvia Burwell. She led the Office of Management and Budget at the White

House and was the mother of two young children, ages four and six. Eventually, she would become the head of HHS and move on to be the president of American University. But it was her high-powered job combined with early motherhood that was the biggest source of wonder.

"The important thing is to focus on delivering impact," she told the women. "Be ruthless about how to prioritize your time and resources. Remember that command of the substance is how you get control of a room. And always deliver. That's what gives you the freedom to take the time you need to be with your kids and raise your family."

That advice was a bit of a head-scratcher for me. Not the "always deliver" part—I get that. If you are given something to do, the person who gave it to you should never have to think about it again until you are reporting back on how the job was completed. It wasn't my experience, though, that always delivering bought me more time with my family.

Reflecting later, I focused more on her emphasis on being ruthless about prioritizing your time. Being highly responsive to the requests and needs of others—as I have always been—can help you succeed *to a point*. Ultimately, though, you have to clarify your own priorities and apply your skills and labor there. Otherwise you risk remaining a bit player in someone else's show.

Some of the best management lessons in the federal government, though, came from my then-boss, Assistant Secretary George Sheldon. He was unusually self-aware, knowing those he needed to surround himself with to fill in for any gaps he had and to do tasks for which he was not suited. A consummate politician—and I say that with respect—he could effectively work any room, deploying his emotional intelligence to consistently make others feel seen and heard.

"Always stop and talk to the people at the front desk and to the administrative assistants," he said. "What they think of you matters, and you need them more than you would think." Sure enough, if George needed to get in to see anyone, he consistently had an advocate among the assistants and that person would make the meeting happen.

Frequently, when I asked his opinion about something, he immediately turned the question back to me. A discussion would ensue, but the decision on how to proceed would be mine. Always, he emphasized, delegate decision making as much as possible. Allowing decisions to be made at the lowest possible level creates greater initiative, drive, and productivity.

One day, after 5 p.m., George stood in my doorway, coat on and hat in hand, waiting for me to wrap up so we could go out for a drink. I was on the phone wrestling with HHS and the White House on a media response, and there was no small amount of handwringing over what, exactly, I was to say to the reporter. At this point George delivered the best communication advice possible:

"Just pick up the phone and tell the truth."

By the close of the Obama administration, management advice took on a different and specific tone.

In January 2016, ACF political appointees were gathering for one final retreat at the Lincoln Cottage, a 250-acre campus at the top of a hill just a few miles north of the White House. The Lincolns resided there a good part of the year to escape the actual and political heat around the White House.

"Focus relentlessly," former ACF assistant secretary Olivia Golden, who served in the Clinton administration, told the ACF appointees. "Pick your top priority and mobilize the agency to embed that priority. Build external buy-in and create capacity in key career leadership positions."

The concern that you weren't spending your time doing what was most important was constant as an appointee, but it was even more urgent in the final year. You could literally count the days left to do the job that you came to do.

Olivia's advice was spot on. We had long worked to put strong leaders in career federal roles. In that last year we moved to bring in those career leaders and influential outside partners, such as leaders of philanthropy, so that they could carry on key initiatives when the Obama administration was over.

With all of our leadership and management efforts, we were reaching for legacy—to put systems and people in place that would keep performing optimally after we were gone. Ultimately, that's the goal of all good management.

LESSON LEARNED

Seek out those who have different or more experiences than you. Listen and learn, but always know your own priorities.

34

Working with the White House, or Not

Few things in Washington are more coveted than getting a meeting at the White House. Those of us who moved to Washington from somewhere else were there, largely, to make a difference. And the assumption is that the most direct route to making that difference sits at 1600 Pennsylvania Avenue. If you are at a meeting there—and "there" includes the Eisenhower Executive Office Building (EEOB) and a handful of historic row houses on Lafayette Square—you have arrived at your destination. Or so you hope.

I attended my first White House meeting in September of 2011, six months after I joined the administration. That morning, I sat in the storied Old Ebbitt Grill on 15th Street with two of my colleagues, Earl Johnson, from the US Office of Family Assistance, and Vicki Turetsky, from the US Office of Child Support Enforcement.

We drank coffee and discussed our shared objective for the conversation with the White House Domestic Policy Council staff about a change in approach to child support. The revised goal of the child support office, we advocated, should be to help fathers get in a position where they can pay child support, not punish them for failing to do so when they had no money. Vicki even wanted to change the name of the office, taking out the word "enforcement."[9] Considerable evidence supported the fact that if fathers had a relationship with and regularly interacted with their kids, they would be more likely to pay child support. Punishing those not paying child support by withholding visitation rights was counterproductive and bad for children and families.

All three of us were in our 50s, with decades of experience in our respective work. With Obama in the White House and all of us in senior political appointments, this was a moment to access and use power for positive policy change. Lingering too long, we had to rush out of Old Ebbitt to be on time for our early meeting. Our waiter knew why we were there and where we were going. He didn't bother to bill us for our coffee. "You'll be back," he said. (He was right.)

We ended up meeting in one of the row houses on Lafayette Park across from the White House. We met with three policy staff focused on fatherhood work. They were all about 25 years old, sporting exemplary social skills and suits. We talked and they politely listened but had nothing of substance to share. We left with the realization that what progress we would make was going to be up to us.

It was an early lesson—often reinforced—about the limitations of a functional relationship with the White House. I eventually learned to be discerning about which White House meetings I would attend, my decisions based largely on the agenda and who would be in the room. For every invitation to a White House meeting, one had to submit information for advance security clearance. Then, an hour prior to the scheduled start, you went to the White House, queued up outside the guard gate, and started the laborious security process. (It was much like visiting a prison, except you got to keep your jewelry on.) A meeting at the White House invariably would cost half a working day, an eternity for a political appointee working under a relentlessly ticking clock.

But White House ceremonial functions were a particular bonus for political appointees. The summer staff picnic, the Christmas tours, the Easter Egg Roll. These were all moments you got to just look around and think: I get to be here. Adjacent, at least, to the inheritors of history and holders of power. As corny as it might seem, it tapped into my well of American sentimentality. I would think of my great-grandfather, who signed his naturalization papers in Pittsburgh with an X. Or my Ireland-born grandmother, who had little formal education and gave birth to six children at home. Or my father, whose fingernails were perpetually so stained from auto grease that he would regularly hide them under the table at more formal events. And me, now? *I get to be here.*

$\boxtimes$

In 2012 President Obama was preparing for his annual address to staff. The years prior, he spoke to staff via a voice conference call. This year he wanted to have staff in the room. The White House liaisons in each department were asked to select representatives from each operational division to go to the White House, where Obama would address a small group of political appointees while the rest of them would phone in.

I had just finished launching an enormous website for ACF. With customized sections for each of the 12 major program offices, the site took a year to build and had thousands of pages and dozens of unique functionalities. It also launched ACF's new branding and logo—actually the first and only branding and logo the agency had ever had. Mike Mc-Cauley, the HHS White House liaison, was impressed with the breadth and speed of the work, so he asked me to represent ACF at the White House for this event.

It was the most singular recognition I had ever received for my work. I remember riding my bike home from work the day I learned I would be going to this event with Obama, wishing my father was still alive so that I could tell him. Mom was certainly proud, but Dad? Dad, whose own father made him promise to never vote for a Republican because he, my grandfather, held Republicans responsible for the Depression? Dad would have cried.

When the day came for Obama's address to staff, I slogged through the laborious security process and filed into the South Court Auditorium, which was directly adjacent to the West Wing of the White House. I found a seat on the aisle, still nurturing a fantasy that Obama and I would actually interact, or that he would see me and recognize me from working together when I was with SEIU and he was in the Illinois State Senate.

It was January 30—Jack Lew's first day as chief of staff, replacing Bill Daley, who had replaced Rahm Emanuel. Lew and several other senior White House staff greeted us, focusing on the upcoming State of the Union address and what we could all do to amplify key messages.

And then the president entered, and we all stood. He said to pass along his apologies to our families for all the soccer games and family events missed and for all the checking of our Blackberrys while on vacation.

"You will never be in a better position to help more people in your entire career than you are right now," he said to the few dozen of us in the room and the thousands of appointees listening in on the call. "We have staffed our government with extraordinary people. You help keep our kids safe and our environment sound. In the abstract, people get down on government, but when they need help and we come through they appreciate it. You are all helping make government a force for good."

He was great. Even if he didn't see me—or anyone else most likely given how the stage was lit. He delivered the message that appointees needed to hear.

It was never long, though, before the sublime swung back to the ridiculous. Every time the "White House" reached out to people at the department level to support an event, you would end up working with too many people with too little experience, all terrified to make a mistake, but all overly confident from years of being the smartest kid in the class. (The Jonah Ryan character in *Veep*? Spot. On.)

Typically, whatever these charming young staff needed had to be provided instantly. In any other context, arranging details at the last minute would have led to certain failure of any event. But this was the White House. If you called someone in California on a Monday and invited them to a meeting at the White House on Tuesday, they would be on a plane on Monday night.

By two years into what would be nearly six years of service, I had learned to limit my contact with the White House to only activities that were strategically critical to reaching my goals. When they reached out about a June 2013 Champions of Change event related to the children of incarcerated parents, I delegated the project to my able special assistant, Jesse Garcia, and never heard another word about it.

At other times, though, their engagement was less benign. A major policy change during the Obama administration was to open up competition for Head Start contracts, many of which had been held by the same providers for decades, with widely varying performance results.

In early 2013 we had put together a short and simple press release about the second cohort of Head Start providers, who would have to compete with other agencies for their contract. This would be a local story in every city that we listed in the release. Days prior to the announcement, the press release was cleared by the Department of Health and Human Services. Then it went to the White House for approval, where it sat. And sat. Finally, they cleared it 90 minutes before it was scheduled to go out.

One of ACF's public affairs specialists, Ted Froats, was all set to push the release out at 11 a.m. Then, at five minutes to the hour, I got a call from the public affairs shop at HHS: "The policy shop people from the White House are reviewing the release and may have some changes."

I bolted two floors down and got to Ted right before he hit send. Ten minutes later I received the edited version. Someone from the White House had thoughtfully inserted grammatical errors and changed everything out of Associated Press style. Someone must have had an intern with nothing to do. I told Ted to send the previous version.

There were exceptions to this mayhem. When you connected to and worked with a more senior member of staff who provided solid leadership to the young people around them, interactions were more respectful and less manic.

This was true of the Hispanic Roundtable held early in Obama's second term and led largely by Julie Chávez Rodríguez, Cesar Chavez's granddaughter. (Talk about someone likely to have had wistful thoughts about the contrast between her life and the lives of her parents and grandparents.) Many national Hispanic leaders were invited to air their concerns, particularly about the way the government was managing the unaccompanied children coming over the Mexican border. Between the leadership of so many respected Hispanic staff at the Obama White House and the solemn grandeur of the setting—we were in the Indian Treaty Room in the EEOB—the critical voices were more tempered. They left that day with assurance that they had allies in the Obama administration. That day, the White House was used effectively as a powerful persuasive channel with an important constituency.

My favorite White House event, though, was to be my last. Mishaela Durán, the director of regional operations, whom I hired and came to mentor, along with several other of my key staff, organized a goodbye party for me in a large conference room in the Eisenhower Executive Office Building. I still don't know how they pulled it off. Most of our goodbye parties for departing appointees were in bars in the Gallery Place neighborhood.

Weeks before—just prior to the November election of Donald Trump—we had held a large summit of foundation leaders in this same room, aligning agendas so that philanthropy was all set to work with the anticipated Hillary Clinton administration. At my party we tried not to think about how much the world had changed since the last time we had been in that room.

That night, Mishaela had a bar set up in one corner with a specially recruited bartender, Pat McMonagle, from a local Irish pub. Food was arranged on a large table, and a slideshow of photos from my years in the administration, put together by Brendan, who was then 17, played on a large screen at the end of the room.

There were tributes, toasts, laughs, and an enthusiastic amount of drinking in a short amount of time. But the EEOB was no bar, and a couple hours into our party we were told it was time to leave the building.

Two young White House staffers were charged with escorting us out after we packed up all our supplies and loaded up the boxes of beverages on a dolly. We drunkenly meandered through the marble hallways, wrestling the dolly down wide steps and getting repeatedly distracted by artwork and historic markers. A straggler or two would start wandering down a different hallway, much to our escorts' dismay.

It probably took us close to 30 minutes to leave the building, with the young staffers getting increasingly frustrated at being ignored. It was a good note on which to end my relationship with these bright young stars of the Washington, DC, workforce.

It was December 2016. We bid the White House one last, tipsy goodbye.

LESSON LEARNED

Power doesn't always reside where you think it does. Don't just look up for power; look all around you.

Part Six

Never Stop Learning

35

Coming Home to a City So Real

Ten intense years had passed since we left Chicago. Brendan was finishing third grade when we moved out of our two-flat on the south side, and now he was in his first year of college. I had never wanted to leave Chicago, and now my desire to return was tinged with desperation. I wanted the Oz-like skyline on the massive expanse of Lake Michigan, the classy jazz clubs, the gritty blues clubs, the quirky theater scene, the miles of flat bike lanes, the beaches with trees, the parks with music, the restaurants with no limits to the elevation of bar food and every ethnic cuisine imaginable.

And the people. The roughly even mix of Black, Brown, and white with endless new groups of immigrants. Together they created an American history of class and race struggle that ranged from the positive—the most founding locals (Local 1) of craft and industrial unions in the country—to the tragic—the 1919 race riots where 38 people died and more than 1,000 Black families were left homeless due to arson. It was the city that burned down in 1871 and rebuilt better in two years. It was the city that in 1900 reversed the flow of its own river to protect the drinking water of Lake Michigan from its own filth. (Sorry Saint Louis.)

For all of its flashy presence and collective accomplishments, though, Chicago was still midwestern. Friendly, modest. You didn't hear much about the "smartest people in the room" here. It would imply everyone else in the room wasn't as smart, which would be rude. And it was a welcoming city. It has been said that if your layover was long enough at O'Hare, Chicagoans would accept you as a local.

Nelson Algren compared loving Chicago to "loving a woman with a broken nose. You may find lovelier lovelies, but never a lovely so real."[1]

Alex Kotlowitz, in one of his numerous wonderful books, adapted that for
his book about Chicago: *Never a City So Real.*[2]

Chicago was also home to Jeff's family, which reflected the immigrant history of the city, with his father's Jewish family emigrating from
Poland in the early 1900s. Bernie Epton, Jeff's dad, served as a navigator
in World War II, where he met Audrey Issett at a military social function
in England in 1944. Audrey was a native of London serving as a plane
spotter in the British military. With Audrey at his side, Bernie became a
prominent insurance attorney and Illinois state legislator as they raised
four children in Chicago. Bernie eventually played a conspicuous role in
the city's history of racial conflict. In 1983, in a campaign charged with
racism, he ran against Harold Washington, who was to become Chicago's
first Black mayor. Jeff's father died four years before we married, so I
never knew him. But Audrey, my mother-in-law, had become my friend,
and Jeff's siblings, nieces, and nephews had become my second family.

And then there were my foster kids. The five surviving girls all lived
in and around Fort Wayne, just a three-hour drive from Chicago. I had
stayed close to two of them: Molly, the fourth of the six siblings, and Josie,
the youngest. They each had one daughter, with whom I was also close.
We would regularly get together at least once a year when I was in DC.
Now, we would be able to see each other more frequently.

The White House was generous with those of us who were staying until the end of the administration. We had lots of professional guidance
on everything from resume preparation to networking for job hunting.
I built an elaborate list of all my contacts in Chicago and planned several networking and interview trips throughout 2016. Through Obama
colleague contacts I ended up having a private meeting with Illinois Supreme Court judge Anne Burke and lunch with Diana Rauner, an early
childhood development expert who was married to then-Governor Bruce
Rauner. I visited major foundations and nonprofits throughout the city. I
set up breakfasts, lunches, and dinners with everyone I knew and some
I didn't know who could have connections to organizations in which I
would want to work.

It became very clear that communications jobs and leadership roles in progressive nonprofits were more plentiful and better paid in DC than in Chicago. I was approached by headhunters about senior communication roles based in DC and New York and did an initial interview for VP of communications for Planned Parenthood, just in case they would budge on their Manhattan-office requirement. They wouldn't.

I ended up with a clear choice between being the national comms director for an education reform organization, which had an office in Chicago and three other cities, or working in the area of child welfare with several Obama administration colleagues. Public school reform and child welfare intersected with both my professional and personal lives. Ultimately, the deciding factor was the experience and maturity of the leadership and senior staff at Chapin Hall at the University of Chicago, where three other Obama alumni landed and where one, Bryan Samuels, served as the executive director. Chapin Hall focuses on research and policy related to child and family well-being, with a substantial research portfolio related to foster youth and a growing body of work related to youth homelessness. The position also had the advantage of limited travel. After spending four of my six years in the Obama Administration overseeing 10 regional offices, I was ready to spend a lot less time in hotels.

In my social and professional circles, the atmosphere in DC after Donald Trump was elected and before he was inaugurated was one of despair. The monuments and buildings around the city that had always moved me now gave me a sense of dread. Most federal staff were shaken and worried. This was not a normal change from one party to another. The Trump administration felt like a massive freight train moving at full speed while the country sat on the tracks just ahead. I had to look away.

I was engaged in the frenzied closing of the administration while we were selling our DC home and preparing to move. Jeff traveled to Chicago, where he found us a temporary apartment in Hyde Park. On Friday, January 20, 2017, Donald Trump was inaugurated. The next Monday, I started my new job as communication director at Chapin Hall.

I dug into my work building a communication infrastructure and team at Chapin Hall while reestablishing a home and social life in Chicago. Before long I started enjoying the decidedly different work culture.

Happy hour dynamics illustrate this difference. In DC, if you scheduled a happy hour among colleagues for 6 p.m., most people wouldn't show up until 7. The remainder would text you and say they couldn't make it because they were still working. In Chicago, happy hours are scheduled for 4 p.m., and if you don't show up until 6, everyone will be gone because they have gone home to have dinner with their families. And if you repeatedly don't show up because you are working through these happy hours, people will start worrying about you. They may arrange an intervention.

I left Chicago in 2007 because of a unique opportunity—to work with one of history's most innovative labor leaders (Andy Stern) at a time when we were about to have our first African American president. I am forever grateful that Jeff was willing to leave so much behind for this opportunity. But I came to learn how important it was to live where you know you want to be. Good work is everywhere. And as we've seen through living through the pandemic, good work can be done anywhere.

It's important to find your happy place, commit to it, and settle into it. Particularly if there's a storm that you need to ride out. And, boy, were big storms coming.

LESSON LEARNED

To move forward, you may have to go where you don't really want to be. But if there is a place that is close to your heart, find a way back there.

36

Building a Communications Team

It had been more than a dozen years since I had been on the back end of a website. That's where you enter the copy, arrange the images, choose the font size for the headlines. In all of my DC jobs, there were people who did only that. Teams of people, usually. My previous comms and external affairs teams had ranged from 5 people to nearly 100.

At Chapin Hall at the University of Chicago, though, I *was* the communication shop. I had access to one person, Matt Brenner, who was half-time on communications—mostly editing and posting the reports we produced. The other half of his job was providing administrative support to the chief of staff and to building services. Loyal and diligent, Matt had been there for nearly 20 years and had the most potluck job description I had ever seen.

Communications is labor intensive. Having people available to consistently produce messages in a variety of ways—social media posts, videos, targeted emails, data visualizations—is much more effective than having a lot of money to, say, buy paid advertising or outside consulting. Once you apply a strategic framework like the Persuasion Matrix and create a detailed communication plan, you will be looking at a lot of work. Without the right number of people with the right skills at the table, the work simply can't be done.

When I came to Chapin Hall, I wasn't just place shopping; I was boss shopping. During four years of the Obama administration, Bryan Samuels led the Administration for Children, Youth and Families, one of the program offices of the Administration for Children & Families, where I served in the executive office as a deputy assistant secretary. (Two other colleagues from the Obama administration, Clare Anderson and Sonali Patel, had also come to Chapin Hall.) Bryan was smart, thoughtful, and informed by lived experience; a native of Chicago's south side, he had spent most of his childhood in congregate care. He was also a strong speaker, and an excellent media interview, and those who worked for him confirmed that he was the opposite of a micromanager. I respected him and knew he was someone I could work for and with.

Bryan was not, however, ever focused on communications. He had no social media accounts, was not a writer, and had little experience supervising communication functions. But the organization under Bryan's leadership was growing, and the communications needs were expanding with it. Chapin Hall's website was dated, social media channels were not established, media response was minimal, and proactive media work was nonexistent. The many experts on staff were increasingly demanding better.

A reputable research center with a $20 million–plus operating budget, more than 120 staff, and lots of good information to share needed a strong communication function. But it didn't have so much as a file of photos or a single media list. No product templates, no data visualization or video capacity, no media-monitoring service, certainly no branding guide or identity standards. The communication shelves were empty.

There are times when communication leaders are in a position to build a shop from scratch, such as when working at a start-up, at an organization that is being reorganized, or at one that is growing rapidly. Bryan was actively and consciously changing Chapin Hall and pushing for an approach that engaged youth and families in research; he also worked directly with practitioners and policymakers to apply the research. Even though Chapin Hall had been around for 35 years, he saw his version of the organization as a start-up. So that's how I approached building the communication shop. Over five years, I followed a three-step process to build a strong shop that supported the new vision for Chapin Hall.

STEP ONE: DEFINE WHAT IS NEEDED FOR A STRONG COMMUNICATION SHOP

Think big, but be clear on the foundational priorities. To illustrate everything we needed, I used PowerPoint to draw a house made of boxes

The Components of a Communication Operation

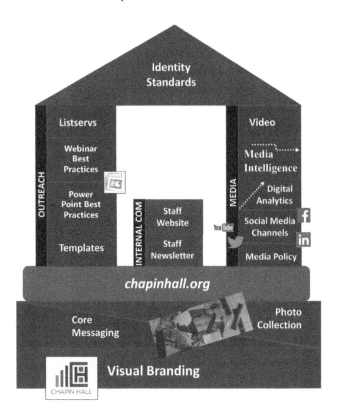

Figure 2: Elements of Chapin Hall's Communication Infrastructure

(see figure 2). Its foundation included visual branding, core messaging, and a photo collection. We needed those things first before we built anything else.

Immediately on top of that foundation was the website, which had to be modern, attractive, and highly searchable. Our goal to be on the cutting edge of applied research had to be reflected in our website design and content.

On that foundation I added three "wings" to the house.

The Outreach wing: templates for products, presentations, and visualizations; email lists; standards for webinars and PowerPoints.

The internal comms wing: the staff website and newsletter.
The media wing: outreach lists, monitoring and clippings, social media, and video production.

And then on top of all of those wings was the broadest piece that served as the roof: identity standards. When we started, almost all of these blocks in this structure were gray, which indicated they didn't exist. Within three years, the boxes were all filled in with our brand colors, burgundy and deep blue, to signify they were in place.

STEP TWO: DETERMINE WHO AND WHAT ARE NEEDED TO FULFILL THE FUNCTIONS DEFINED IN STEP ONE

Some work, such as branding and identity development, can be done by outside firms. Some, such as media monitoring and list development, can be provided by a service. Other work can be done by freelancers, such as profile shots of your staff and other original photography. PR firms can do episodic media events. But the most powerful approach is strong staffing: a group of people who, day in and day out, are promoting your organization. All of that support might not be available initially, so understanding other options for getting the work done is essential.

STEP THREE: DETERMINE YOUR IDEAL STEADY-STATE STAFFING PLAN

Considering everything you laid out in the first two steps, what is your ideal staffing plan? This plan is aspirational, but it is based on your communications expertise and the best interest of your organization. If you were to fire on all communication cylinders and get your organization's message out daily through all available channels, what would your staff look like? Which people with which skills would carry out which functions? Draw up your dream staff flowchart. That's your vision. Be ready to share it at any and all staffing and budget discussions. When someone expresses a communication need, you have something to point to and say: *this* is what I need to do *that*.

Persuasion research is clear on what it takes to influence someone to make a decision that you want them to make. In this case, you are trying to convince organizational decision-makers—a board, an executive director, a senior management team—to invest in communication capacity. The four fundamentals of persuasion messages are relative advantage, compatibility, complexity, and trialability or observability. Your messages would have to clarify the advantages of communication capacity to the organization, why that capacity is compatible with the organization's mission, and why, in your hands, that capacity is not overly complex. And you need to take your organization on a trial run: either with a demonstration project where you show the power of communications with a specific project, or through looking at what other organizations who invest in communications can do.

At Chapin Hall, evidence talks. So I needed to gather some to get more senior staff and leadership on the communication bandwagon. I chose five other research centers that had quality communication materials. They included large, well-known national organizations like Mathematica, the Pew Charitable Trusts, and the Brookings Institution, and two University of Chicago–affiliated institutions: NORC and the Consortium on School Research. I reviewed their materials, compiling links to their most compelling products, and interviewed their communication directors.

I charted each organization's total staffing and their communication staffing to determine a ratio. At Pew Charitable Trust and the Consortium, the ratio was roughly 1 communication staff person to every 8 staff. At Mathematica—with a comms department of 100 people—the ratio was 1 comms person for every 12 staff. At Chapin Hall our ratio was 1 comms staff for every *80* staff.

Growth was a theme across all of these organizations. "It takes a lot more people to be engaged in discussion of all of our core issues on multiple platforms than it took to just publish reports," said Melissa Skolfield, who was the vice president of communications at Pew Charitable Trusts and had previously led communications for Brookings. While a decade earlier it was routine to post a report and write a press release about it, now you had to develop content for all social media channels, develop a video, and host a webinar. That takes people.

David Roberts at Mathematica emphasized the same. "It used to be that publishing in an academic journal was adequate. Now, so much more is expected," he said. "If you are just in academic journals, you won't be seen as a thought leader and a go-to source for media and policy makers. To get to that place, you need media, social content, videos, followers, speaking engagements, blogs. It takes moving on a lot of channels to be seen as a player or an influencer."

I had been at Chapin Hall for two years when my 20-page report on comparative organizations' communication capacity was completed and circulated. Each of the next three years, I was able to add one staff person per year, while also making my half-time person full time in communications. Jasmine Jackson transformed our ability to do data visualizations and added video capacity. Isabelle Cadrot was to be the efficient project manager and social media innovator we so desperately needed. Last, we were able to hire an experienced writer and media relations person, Colleen Sharkey, who could implement critical proactive media relations and writing projects targeted to public officials and the press. With a staff of five, we could finally deliver.

In the Communication Network, a national professional communication organization, single communication staff are called "lone wolves." One of the most unfair dynamics I see in communications is when these lone wolves, or shops not much bigger than that, are compared to and expected to achieve results similar to well-funded and -staffed communication shops. If something isn't happening in communications, the most likely reason is that no one was hired to do it.

Fight for the capacity you need in the most strategic way possible. If you don't get it, do what you can, but carefully manage the expectations of others who have no business expecting a staff of one to do the work of five.

I still work in the back end of our website. Web maintenance platforms are much more user-friendly than they were 15 years ago. It's fun to build a page—adding images, graphics, pull quotes—make it go live, and start driving traffic to it. I'm a little obsessed with our web analytics dashboard. We send a promotional email about a page, and I check to see what traffic that created. We post on Twitter (now X), and I look to see how many hits that drew.

It's all practicing the craft. And gathering information for the next time. Every day we are learning, always learning.

LESSON LEARNED

To build a communication team from the ground up, clearly define what the organization needs and the team members it will take to meet those needs. Then fight for those resources.

37

Twittersphere

I had been active on Twitter for years before I posted something that could even come close to being considered viral. On a spring day in 2022, Chicago mayor Lori Lightfoot had announced a new curfew for teenagers after one young person shot and killed another downtown in Millennium Park.

Soon after the announcement I posted: "Let's talk about what to do for Chicago's youth that doesn't involve curfews, chaperones, and criminalization. Here's one: keep parks open late like they did in LA." Then I inserted a clipping with a graphic about the Los Angeles Summer Lights program. "Here's another," I added in a comment to the first post. "Those kids with huge social media followings who are mobilizing young people to gather? Put THEM on a blue ribbon commission and ask them what activities they'd like to mobilize for that we can all live with and where we can keep them safe."

Then I went into a Zoom meeting, emerging an hour later to see more retweets and likes for this post than I had ever had before. The timing, combined with capturing a common sentiment about Mayor Lightfoot's consistent ham-handedness, drove the response. Ultimately, it had more than 150 retweets, nearly 700 likes, and more than 32,000 impressions. That may be chump change compared to stuff that's really viral, but in my little corner of Twitter, and for a 61-year-old woman still figuring out this platform, it was the big time. At this point, I had been active on Twitter for nearly three years. While I oversaw the Twitter account for Chapin Hall, I knew I wouldn't really understand this channel unless I immersed myself in my own account.

Understanding new channels is nonnegotiable for a professional communicator. If there's a tool to reach an audience, you have to know how to use it. I joined Twitter in 2009 when it had 18 million users (@marrianne). By 2019, when I started more actively using the channel, it had grown to 368 million users. The growth in this and other social media channels also changed communication shops. Organizations and individuals pivoted to controlling and feeding their own channels rather than relying on the press to circulate and amplify messages. When my career started, there were dozens of markets of millions—major TV networks, radio stations, and newspapers. Now, though, there are millions of markets of dozens. This sea change was driven by social media.

Twitter has always stood out among other social media channels when it comes to social influence. It has become the town square that journalists use to gauge public sentiment. Not unlike, and certainly no more scientific, than the random "man on the street" interviews that journalists once did. While the platform has no shortage of cranks and trolls, it is disproportionately occupied by influencers.

It is also the opposite of mass media: millions of individuals control their own small channels. An individual with a Twitter account who gets a retweet from a dozen people with good followings can reach more people than they can with a piece published in a midsized daily. And the audience would likely be much better targeted to those you might want to reach about a specific topic.

In 2019 I bought a book on Twitter strategy and read a slew of articles on best practices with the channel. I built up my own following by following others, unfollowing those who didn't follow back. I identified accounts that had content most similar to mine—progressive social commentary about Chicago, bicycling, local architecture, Democratic politics—and scrolled through their followers looking for people to follow. I would follow dozens of people at a time in hopes of picking up at least a fraction of them as followers. I planned numerous posts on different topics, jumped into active conversations, live-tweeted from events, posted photos of sunrises and breaking news.

The unavoidable conclusion after a couple years of conscious and thoughtful tweeting: Twitter (now X) is a tough room. Generally, a half-dozen interactions would feel like a success. It still does. Unlike on

Facebook and Instagram, no one is going to like or share something to be sociable. Agreeability doesn't characterize this channel. And it takes time to build up followers, which of course determines how many feeds your tweet shows up in.

I found that, particularly as I was building my account, it was easier to get more impressions by jumping into a current conversation—particularly if it is on a chain of someone with tens of thousands of followers. In 2021 former secretary of education Arne Duncan (50K+ followers) challenged Chicago police about how they deal with young Black men, referring specifically to an incident involving teenagers who were out in the middle of the night. I responded that my friends and I avoided police when we snuck out at night as teenagers, noting that we did so not because we thought they would arrest us or shoot us but because we thought they would take us home. I wrote it quickly in response to what Arne had posted, and it contained a grammatical error, but up until that time it was my post with the most engagements. Again: timing plus meaningful content was the winning combination.

Early in 2020 I was at my desk at work at Chapin Hall when a call came in from my youngest foster daughter's daughter, Angela, who was 15 at the time. She was hysterical, screaming. I thought for sure that she was being attacked, and I couldn't understand what she was saying. She was finally able to slow down and lower her voice enough that I could understand her.

Her mother, Josie, had collapsed in the living room of their home. The paramedics had been called and were there. Angela called me at the point when it was clear that they weren't able to revive her immediately. They put Josie on a stretcher and took her into the ambulance, and Angela and her stepfather rushed behind to the hospital.

The oldest Martin girl, Norah, lived nearby. She had recently gotten clean and remarried. She, too, rushed to the hospital along with other family nearby. They let me know they were in the waiting room standing by. As they saw the doctor approaching, they dialed me up and put me on speaker phone so that I could hear the update with them.

I could hear the doctor quietly saying, "I'm sorry," after which I could

only hear Angela crying out. She was a 15-year-old only child with no relationship with her biological father, and now her mother was gone. Josie,
who suffered a range of health problems her entire adult life, died of heart
failure at only 39. I quickly checked in with Bryan, my boss, went home,
packed a few things, and rushed down to Fort Wayne.

On November 6, 2020, the Friday after Joe Biden beat Donald Trump in
the presidential election, social media channels were still buzzing with
election discussion. When Khary Penebaker (@kharyp), the treasurer
of the Democratic National Committee Black Caucus and an elector in
Wisconsin, posted about the importance of Black support for Biden, I
responded with the following: "Black people built this country, and now
they are going to save it. In the next administration, we need to prioritize
gratitude for that."

I tend to post early in the morning not because it's good strategy but
because that's when I'm reading the newspaper and catching up with my
social media accounts. Many of these early morning posts (this one was at
5:43 a.m.) don't get many impressions, but this one did. The most chilling
was an early retweet by an account that has since been suspended. It only
said: "You know what to do." A white-supremacist Twitter storm ensued:

"Lies . . . how could they build the US when they never managed to
build Africa."

"The white Europeans built this nation. Overwhelmingly. In every
aspect."

"You are a very stupid and ignorant person if you actually believe
this."

And so on. Going back to look at it two years later, many of the respondents have since had their accounts suspended, so these aren't even
the worst comments. My nephew and son jumped in and started a coun-
terattack, which was a little fun to watch. I tried to stick to calmly correct-
ing misinformation. No, contrary to what respondents declared, I don't
live in an all-white suburb; I've lived in majority Black and Brown urban neighborhoods most of my adult life. But there's a limit to engaging
with hostile posters. It's pointless to engage with someone who publicly
professes his ignorance about the role of Black people in building the

powerhouse economy and artistic culture of the United States. I'm not going to convert him through Twitter. Feeding trolls on this platform only strengthens them.

These are some of my key lessons from Twitter: be challenging and provocative in a timely way, get into discussions with people who have lots of followers, gain followers by following. But here's the most important one: be your best self. You will see many posts to which it is tempting to respond with something as caustic as it is thin. Always stop and consider: Is this your best public self? Will this really add to the discussion in a pro- ductive way, or is it just self-indulgent? It's hard to resist when you want to say something inappropriate that you know will get a lot of positive response. But, for the sake of the civility on this platform and your own image, please do.

"Live as if you were to die tomorrow," Mahatma Gandhi said. "Learn as if you were to live forever." In communications, you need to learn as if you will *work* forever. While the principles of audience targeting, message reinforcement, and commitment to accuracy remain constant, the tactics for executing those principals are always evolving. And we've all got to keep up.

LESSON LEARNED

New channels and tools in communication will keep emerging. Keep up. Learn them all.

38

The Promise and Peril of AI

The ground shifted under the communications profession in October 2022. That's when OpenAI's ChatGPT became publicly available, free, and ridiculously easy to use. With detailed, carefully constructed prompts entered into the app, a user could quickly get a solid first draft of a range of products. Enter a press release, and get a half-dozen social media posts. Enter a resume, and get a written bio. Enter a new workplace policy, and get an all-staff email introducing it. *In seconds.*

Most of us will likely remember our first OMG moment with AI. Mine was with my communication staff at Chapin Hall when we were struggling under the weight of a particularly demanding internal team. As we were meeting and discussing this challenge, Gen Z staffer Isabelle Cadrot entered some details about problematic dynamics with this staff team in the ChatGPT prompt and asked it to craft an email to them to address those issues. The email was specific, direct, and professional but brutally blunt. While we howled with delight, the impolitic directness lacked emotional intelligence and would have provoked unproductive confrontation. It was immediately clear that a conversation, not an email, was a superior next step. Still, we were wowed.

At a meeting soon after that one, I told my team that I was working on jacket copy for this book. Once again, Isabelle put in a prompt—"Write book jacket copy for 'Noble Causes and Bruising Battles: Lessons from a career in communication.'" (This was the initial working title of the book.) Again, in seconds, out it came. "As a seasoned communications professional, Jessica Brown has seen it all. In her new book she shares her wealth of experience and insights gained over a career spanning two decades."

So, a few things. First, if ChatGPT doesn't have a piece of information (like author name and years of experience), it just makes something up. It's like a brilliant, sycophantic, pathological liar. No matter what you ask AI to do, it will quickly and eagerly give you an answer, even if it has to completely invent it. That's why your prompts have to be thorough. Second, it is riddled with clichés. (Seen it all. Wealth of experience.) That's not an unusual characteristic of any first draft, but it requires rewriting to make it authentic. Third, there were likely whole sentences in this copy that were pulled from other book jackets. ChatGPT plagiarizes shamelessly and doesn't tell you when it is doing so.

I finished writing my first draft of the jacket copy the old-fashioned way—out of my head. I was afraid to be somehow contaminated by what ChatGPT would produce. But then I went back to Chat and entered a more fleshed out prompt: several paragraphs from my book proposal. It did much better. The language was still a bit too, well, *excited*. (Remarkable career, must-read, handbook for success.) But it was instructive—it captured the tone and style of the marketing language of a book jacket, the 250 words designed to sell the 60K+ words between the covers. The ChatGPT examples helped orient me to that style.

Since our initial experiments, we have started to use ChatGPT more routinely. The initial work to carefully craft language is still in the communicator's court. But once you have done that, it can help you quickly create ancillary materials. With strong top-line messaging and talking points, ChatGPT can create first drafts of social media posts, press releases, video scripts, emails to targeted audiences. Used well, it can greatly accelerate workflow.

"I don't think communications jobs are under threat by AI. But your job may be under threat by people who best know how to use AI," said Alistair Wheate, a senior solution strategist for Brandwatch during a spring 2023 webinar sponsored by Cision. "You can't just put your fingers in your ears. Throw yourself into it."

Investment in AI is increasing and its uses expanding. Businesses have already been using chatbots to interface with customers. Streaming services use it to determine what you would most like to watch. Attorneys are using it to write first drafts of briefs and motions. This isn't a fad.

Is it scary? Yes. Historian Richard Rhodes, writing about the range of technological developments that emerged during the Spanish Civil War in the 1930s, said: "If destructive technology amplifies violence, constructive technology amplifies compassion."[3] He was comparing the destructive development of large-scale aerial warfare to the constructive development of accurate blood typing and battlefield blood transfusions. AI has the potential to be constructive *and* destructive—from delivering us from tedious tasks to potentially independently deciding to wage war. It is already doing the former, and preventing the latter will require that the process of building guard rails around generative AI will outpace its development. An increasing number of experts are warning that we are already behind in constructing those rails.[4]

In communications, AI-generated misinformation can create real-world consequences. On May 22, 2023, an AI-generated forgery of a photo of the Pentagon on fire led to a drop in the stock markets, which corrected after the image was identified as fake.[5] The implications for reliability of information are profound: you will literally not be able to believe what you see. Deep fakes will look authentic. The media literacy required to separate fact from fiction will be higher than ever, as will the ethical demands on communication professionals.

There's no telling how much more the ground will shift with these large language models between the writing and the printing of this book. I will be using AI and tracking its development, but I'll also be closely following the work of Timnit Gebru,[6] an expert in the technology who understands its many ethical and social implications. Go forward cautiously, and decide whom you most trust to be your guide in this new space.

LESSON LEARNED

Use ChatGPT and other AI apps to decrease time spent on repetitive tasks and increase your productivity, but make sure your prompts are thorough and always carefully edit AI-generated copy.

39

The Persuasion Plan

Storytelling is effective communication. That's why this book is constructed as a series of narratives from my career and life. But before you can even know what stories to tell—let alone by whom and through which channels—you have to be clear about what you want to happen as a result. That is strategy. This chapter gives you a framework for developing that strategy.

The study of persuasion is extensive; decades of research point to how people adopt new ideas and are persuaded to adopt specific practices. Everett M. Rogers's *Diffusion of Innovations* is the most classic of the texts on this topic and should be on every communicator's bookshelf.[7] *Public Communications Campaigns*,[8] by Ronald E. Rice and Charles K. Atkin, is a communication text that applies these theories to public communication campaigns and analyzes their effectiveness. Content in these texts greatly informed my Persuasion Matrix. (I frequently refer to the matrix as seven years of graduate work in one slide.)

From the Matrix I developed a workbook, which can be used to develop a strategic communication plan. The workbook poses six key questions. Answering them can make all the difference in achieving measurable results.

QUESTION ONE: WHAT IS THE DESIRED OUTCOME?

In setting the outcome, be specific and concrete, make it measurable, make it meaningful, make it possible. The goal could be the election of a candidate, the passage of a piece of legislation, the recruitment of a specific funder to be a regular supporter, an increase in the number of visitors to your website, the recruitment of new clients. Communications is much more effective if you are clear from the beginning WHY you are communicating. It will also make it obvious if you've been successful.

QUESTION TWO: WHO CAN MAKE THIS HAPPEN?

Once you know what you want to happen, you need to identify who can make it happen. If it's electing a candidate, it's the voters who can make it happen. If it's passing legislation in a specific state, it's state legislators. If it's organizing a union, it's the employees in the workplace. Be specific. Sometimes it's an audience of one. In one compelling campaign, anti-death-penalty activists needed to convince one person—Texas governor Rick Perry, who had presided over more executions than any governor in modern history—to stay an execution. Through thoughtful planning and extensively deployed tactics, they were successful.[9]

As you focus on your audience, you need to keep parsing that audience to be most effective. (Remember the Quakers in chapter 7?) Persuasion theory—particularly the Diffusion of Innovations curve (figure 3)[10]—can help you think this through. In any adoption of a new practice, people fall along the curve below, from innovator to laggard. You are an innovator if you are among the first to do something. That's those of you waiting in line for the next iPhone. An early adopter isn't among the first, but they are right after those innovators. Then, when an innovation follows its course, you get an early majority, followed by the late majority. And then there are the laggards, who may never adopt the innovation.

Think about the last time you adopted a new digital tool at work—a new accounting or expense system, or a shared digital workspace. Most of the time, everyone is supposed to do this at the same time. But they don't, right? They fall along this curve. Some do it right away, most take a few months to get used to it, and then there are some who are still resisting the new practice two years later (the laggards). It's just the way people are.

In your communication campaign, you will waste time and money if you are focusing on the laggards. Think about a political campaign. It would be a poor use of resources to focus on someone on the opposite end of the political spectrum as your candidate. You need to identify the early adopters who will support your candidate, your workplace innovation,

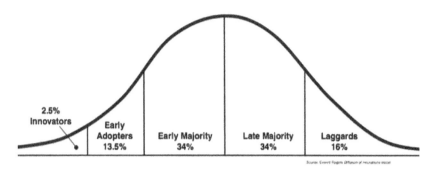

Figure 3: Diffusion of Innovation Theory. Rogers, Everett M. (1995). *Diffusion of Innovations.* Simon and Schuster, New York, *12.*

your service or idea. (In chapter 24, on the thin contract, our focus groups were with potential early adopters—award-winning teachers, teachers at charter schools, Teach for America alumni.)

It's the early adopters who are the key to launching a successful diffusion.

QUESTION THREE: WHY WOULD THEY DO IT?
WHY WOULDN'T THEY?

Now that you've thought carefully about your audience, and who the early adopters are in that audience, it's time to move from who they are to how they might think. Why would your audience want to take the action you want them to take? Why wouldn't they?

This is where polling and focus groups can take the guesswork out of communications. When SEIU was seeking community support for hospital organizing in Chicago, our polling told us the one thing that would most disturb Chicago residents is if a family lost their home due to medical debt. We looked for and found people whose stories captured how atrocious hospital billing and collection practices were.

Effective message framing can also shift over time. For decades, the dominant messaging over cigarette smoking, for example, was a libertarian one: it was a matter of individual choice. But as health consequences and the addictive nature of tobacco became clearer, the frame shifted to one of public health. In a 2004 campaign to raise the cigarette excise tax in Kentucky, organizers conducted focus groups to develop and test messaging.[11] For lawmakers, they determined the most effective messaging was on hidden health-care costs of tobacco use. For women, the best messages were protecting children from smoking and its consequences and how the tax could improve education. The message about familial authority with children, and how the tobacco industry was undermining that with their marketing, proved particularly salient, even in this historically pro-tobacco state. In 2005 Kentucky's cigarette tax went from 3 cents a pack, then the lowest in the nation, to 30 cents a pack.[12]

You don't always need focus groups and polling, though. Sometimes your audience motivation is obvious. For elected officials, getting reelected is a reliable motivator. Local officials need to know that there is support within their own district for what you are advocating and that the issue (and perhaps you and your organization) will work for them in their next election.

There is also considerable publicly available polling on a range of topics that can help you understand your audience better. Those reaching out to the African American community to increase COVID-19 inoculation rates, for example, could easily find key reasons for resistance to the vaccine—which were very different from the reasons that white, rural Christians resisted the vaccine. Those reasons helped shape communication messages and select messengers. The goal of this step is, as much as possible, to get inside the head of your target audience. Don't get stuck in what is persuasive to *you*, because that may not be what is persuasive to your audience.

QUESTION FOUR: WHAT MESSAGES BEST ADDRESS THESE REASONS?

Once you've homed in on your audience and identified the reasons they would or wouldn't support your issue, you are ready to start crafting messages that emphasize why they should be supportive and that address areas of resistance.

As you craft your messages, remember to address these four questions, which, if answered for the audience, lay the groundwork for persuasion:

1. Relative advantage: What advantage does (supporting this candidate, voting for this legislation, adopting this new digital tool) create for me?

2. Compatibility: Is this compatible or consistent with my lifestyle and my values?

3. Complexity: Is it too complicated for me? Tell me how I can manage this so that it isn't overwhelming.

4. Trialability and Observability: Can I see how this works? Can I see the candidate or policy or activity play out in a way that is reassuring?

Also, keep saboteurs in mind. There are competing messengers with competing messages out there. What can inoculate your target audience against these messages without repeating or reinforcing them? (And don't do "myths and facts." Research has found that when myths and facts are presented, the myths are reinforced.)[13]

QUESTION FIVE: WHO ARE THE BEST MESSENGERS FOR THIS AUDIENCE?

Who has the most credibility with your audience? That's who you want delivering the messages. This frequently takes another step or two, but it is well worth it.

Communication polling regularly asks about trusted and influential sources. We know, for example, that medical professionals are much more persuasive messengers on health-care issues than, say, elected officials. And medical professionals who are demographically similar to the target audience are even more persuasive. SEIU polling in 2008 found that nurses were the most trusted professional source overall, so we did a lot of large campaign ads in public spaces with messages from nurses.

In 2021 Chapin Hall conducted a survey of human service providers to determine those they most trust as sources for professional information.[14] People who did the same work as they do were the most credible, followed by their supervisors and agency leadership. If Chapin Hall has evidence that could affect how a child welfare caseworker does her job, for example, Chapin Hall isn't the best messenger for that. Someone she works with is. Consider, again, who the saboteurs might be. Who are the competing and undermining messengers out there? Make sure your messengers are more credible than theirs.

QUESTION SIX: WHAT ARE THE BEST CHANNELS THROUGH WHICH TO REACH THIS AUDIENCE?

How does this audience get their information? What "channels" do they use? That's where you need to deliver and reinforce your messages.

The *National Journal* conducts an annual survey of Capitol Hill influencers to determine where they go to for information that influences their decisions.[15] It surveys Capitol Hill and federal staff and private-sector influencers and asks them what newspapers they read, what social media they use, which TV networks they watch. And it breaks all of that down by party and even where individuals are on the ideological spectrum within their parties. The information is robust and critical for those carrying out campaigns on the Hill. It's not cheap—the full report costs about $4,000—but that's a bargain compared to doing your own polling.

Chapin Hall's survey of human service providers also delved into channels. We found, for example, that those in the youth homelessness advocacy community were particularly active on Twitter, while those in early childhood were very active on Pinterest. As a group, the media outlets human service providers most used were National Public Radio and the *New York Times*, but many of them read local newspapers as well. This and many other details of the survey have allowed us to customize our campaigns based on which audiences we most want to reach.[16]

Communication channels fall along a "richness scale." At one end are the lean communications, which could be a postcard mailer or a tweet from an organizational account. At the other end are the rich communications, the richest of which would be an in-person conversation with someone you know and trust. Everything else—personal social media posts, radio and TV ads, talks at community meetings, flyers at coffee shops—falls along that scale. Some channels have much more power than others, but all are useful for reinforcement.

Think about the last movie you saw in a theater. You might have seen an ad on a bus, read a review in a newspaper, seen a trailer at another movie. All of these are effective at making you think you want to see the movie. But if a good friend with similar taste tells you that you've got to see it, that will be the most powerful influence on you. And repetition here is key: the more ways the message about this movie gets delivered to you, the more likely it is the message will land. The golden rule for message repetition is seven times. Think about how your message is going to get to your target audience no fewer than seven times during your campaign.

Carefully answering all of these questions will allow you to build a genuinely strategic campaign. In communications, the opportunities to waste resources on tactics are endless. All communication directors have to deal with tactical demands outside of strategy. We need an op-ed! We need a TikTok video! We need a story in the *New York Times*! If these demands are taken as directives, the entire communication effort can be subsumed in endless hours of pursing tactics that do not further the campaign goals.

Ask the hard questions, and get results.

LESSON LEARNED

Use what the research has taught us about persuasion to make your communication campaigns as strategic as possible. Avoid wasting time and energy on tactics outside of that strategy.

40

Love What You Do and Love Those You Do It With

In the summer of 1995, when we were still publishing the *Dayton Voice*, the last Martin girl to live with us moved in. The Martin grandparents subscribed to the idea that when you are 18 it's time to leave home. Molly, always the most conscientious and focused of the six girls, had turned 18 in April and graduated from high school in June. She had been accepted at Wilmington College, a small Quaker liberal arts school, but she needed a place to stay through the summer before moving into the dorms. Molly took over the bedroom that three of her sisters had lived in before. I accepted an offer to teach a senior-level communication course at Wilmington, which would have me on campus one evening a week, allowing me to stay in close touch with Molly as she navigated this new world.

There are now only four Martin girls. After the youngest, Josie, died, her daughter, Angela, moved in with her Aunt Molly. She graduated high school and is now working and doing well. Molly had her own daughter, to whom she is fiercely devoted. That daughter graduated from college, is in a committed relationship, and is pursuing a career that she enjoys. The other three Martin girls struggle with addiction and mental health problems, and we only occasionally get word of how they are doing. It's rarely good news. I learned over the years how naive I was to think that my commitment to them could even begin to address the trauma that they endured at being abandoned by their parents. Only one in six, ultimately, is thriving. And Molly is at constant risk of being overwhelmed by the needs of others in her family.

My work now involves translating research and evidence about child welfare to help determine the best practices and policies. When I think about the Martin family in that context, it's clear that the best thing for the family was to work to provide them what they needed to stay together. There were no birth parents to consider—they were gone. But the grandparents might have been able to maintain custody with additional support. I could have provided respite care, taking the kids on weekends to do enriching things, to give the grandparents some relief. Maybe they would have responded to parenting coaching to better manage teenage misbehavior. The girls could have been enrolled in more after-school programs to keep them occupied, out of the house but safe. Additional financial support would have certainly helped. But one thing is clear: taking the girls out of their rural environment where everyone knew them and dropping them into my urban one, rife with new hazards at a vulnerable point in their lives, did them no good.

From the time I worked in my father's gas station as a teenager, my personal and work lives have always been integrated. My love of the Martin girls influenced my career choices—not just short-term decisions like trying teaching, which I enjoyed and plan to do again. But big decisions, like focusing my efforts on what families need to thrive, from better wages and working conditions, to quality public schools and an effective child welfare system. The problems faced by kids who end up in the child welfare system and by low-wage workers aren't communication problems. But communication is always a part of the solution.

During the Obama administration, I visited a jobs program in San Francisco that had identified seemingly minor but important barriers to class mobility. They had a short quiz that they gave everyone when they entered the program, and then they took the same quiz at the end of the program. One of the questions was: "Your cousin comes in to visit from out of town and you have a full-time job. The morning after he arrives do you call in sick or go to work?" At the beginning of the program, everyone said they'd call in sick. At the end, no one did.

When you grow up in a working-class household, you know the rules of work—mainly that you almost always do it. If something bad happens to you, your parents, your spouse or your children, maybe you can miss work. If something happens to your brother-in-law or cousin, not so much. Someone who grows up in a household where the adults did not successfully hold down jobs is less likely to know such nuances.

While I grew up in a working-class, low-income household, both of my parents were strong managers. They always had high and clear expectations at work, while actively caring about the people with whom they worked. What they practiced as common decency is now more commonly understood as creating a positive culture. As the teams I managed grew, so did the effect of building that positive culture. Success at scale comes from creating an environment where everyone can thrive as individuals and be as productive as possible. And enjoy doing it. It's important to manage up to your supervisor, and manage across effectively with peers. But nothing is more central to success, and to day-to-day happiness at work, than managing down well.

Good management requires genuine confidence. It takes a strong sense of yourself to allow others to do things differently than you might do them. To allow others to challenge and disagree with you. To allow others to just show up differently than you do in the world and at work and to be ok with that.

That confidence, being comfortable in your own skin, can override all those smartest people in the room. Soon after Sylvia Burwell was appointed as secretary of HHS during the Obama administration, and after a particularly stressful first couple weeks on the job, she attended a meeting of all the HHS political appointees. She finished her updates and then opened the floor for questions. You could almost smell the sweat of so many appointees trying to craft something brilliant on the spot to impress their new boss. I decided to just speak out. Responding to the emotional intensity of her update, I asked: "How are *you* doing?" She immediately relaxed her posture and started sharing on a more personal level. My question turned out to be the only one raised in that session.

I still see, even now, a type of confidence among my friends from more upper-class backgrounds that I will likely never feel. I see it in my own son, who is finishing law school while starting his work as a public defender. But I know that, even if I don't feel it, there are situations where I have to show unwavering confidence. When no matter who is in the room and what advantages brought them there, my demeanor must be driven by one thought: "I know what I bring to the table, and I can deliver. Just watch me."

LESSON LEARNED

Bring your whole, authentic self to work, and let others do the same.

Notes

INTRODUCTION

1. Dale W. Nelson, *The President Is at Camp David*, foreword by David Eisenhower (Syracuse: Syracuse University Press, 1995).

2. Nelson, *The President Is at Camp David*, 32–50.

3. Nelson, *The President Is at Camp David*, 54.

4. Western Genealogical Society, *A List of Immigrants Who Applied for Naturalization Papers in the District Courts of Allegheny County, PA*, vol. 5, 1981, Protonotary's office, Allegheny County, PA; copies of actual naturalization papers are on microfiche, p. 79.

PART 1

1. Marrianne McMullen, "Gulf and the Spill Cover-Up," *Mountain Journal*, November 1980, 5.

2. Western Genealogical Society, *A List of Immigrants Who Applied for Naturalization Papers in the District Courts of Allegheny County, PA*, vol. 5, 1981, Protonotary's office, Allegheny County, PA; copies of actual naturalization papers are on microfiche.

3. Department of Commerce, Bureau of the Census, Fourteenth Census of the United States: 1920—Population, Pennsylvania, Allegheny County, District number 24, Enumeration district number 837, Ward of Banksville, Sheet No. 9B.

4. McMullen, "Gulf and the Spill Cover-Up."

5. Marrianne McMullen, "Case of the 'SRC-II Hush Up': We May Suffer in a Few Years," *Daily Athenaeum*, December 11, 1980.

6. US Department of Energy, *Remedial Measures Plan for a Spill of Solvent Refined Coal Liquid at the SRC Pilot Plant, Ft. Lewis, Washington: Final Report*, 1980, https://www.osti.gov/biblio/6743994.

7. US Department of Energy, *Remedial Measures*.

8. Alex Jacobs, "Ray Cook, Founder of Native American Journalists Association, Marine Corps Veteran, Dies at 62," *Indian Country Today*, July 20, 2019.

9. Jacobs, "Ray Cook."

10. Jack A. Smith, "My Life and Times with the Guardian," *Rag Blog*, August 2, 2012, http://theragblog.blogspot.com/2012/08/jack-smith-my-life-and-times-with.html.

11. CNN, "CNN Coverage of Space Shuttle Challenger Explosion," January 28, 1986, https://www.youtube.com/watch?v=Yncof4e4tS4.

12. *Daily Athenaeum*, West Virginia University student newspaper, December 9, 1980.

13. "Shuttle Explodes; Crew Feared Dead," *Palladium-Item*, January 28, 1986. (Unsigned photo caption.)

14. Charlotte Ryan and Karen Jeffreys, "Challenging Domestic Violence, Trickle-Up Theorizing about Participation and Power in Communication Activism," in *Communication Activism: Struggling for Social Justice Amidst Difference*, ed. Lawrence R. Frey and Kevin M. Carragee, 3 (New York: Hampton Press, 2007), 185.

PART 2

1. Marrianne McMullen, "Suspending Dayton's Students," January 20, 1994, and "Suspending Children: Are There Other Ways to Deal with Misbehaving Children than Removing Them from School? Many Innovative Educators Think There Are," *Dayton Voice*, January 27, 1994.

2. Martin Yant, "Funny Money at MCCAA: Local Anti-poverty Agency under Investigation for Spending Funds on Gifts, Trips, Food and Legal Settlements," *Dayton Voice*, January 5, 1995.

3. Martin Yant, "The House That David and Raleigh Built: Funds for Low-Income Housing End up in Office Space for 'Friend of David,'" *Dayton Voice*, February 16, 1995.

4. Jeff Epton, "Cops and Doctors: Dr. Dewey Mays' Practice Destroyed by Dayton Police Dept. Overzealous Prosecution," *Dayton Voice*, September 18, 1996.

5. Jeff Epton, "Dr. Dewey Mays Dies, His Backers Still Seek Justice," *Dayton Voice*, July 2, 1997.

6. Jeff Epton, "Lt. David Sherrer Resumes Fight against DPD," July 9, 1997; "Hearing on Sherrer's Firing Concludes; Decision Expected Soon," August 27, 1997; "Sherrer Wins Again; Board Orders Reinstatement," November 24, 1997; "Black Officers Back Sherrer during Internal Affair Probe," October 15, 1997; "More than Money: City Apologizes to David Sherrer," February 11, 1999—all in the *Dayton Voice*.

7. McMullen, "Suspending Children," *Dayton Voice*, January 27, 1994.

8. McMullen, "Suspending Children."

9. Marrianne McMullen, "Voice Moves to Santa Clara," *Dayton Voice*, November 15, 1995.

10. Marrianne McMullen, "Streetwalkers," *Dayton Voice*, February 26, 1997.

11. Marrianne McMullen, "Music Awards Recognize Ohio Players, Lester Bass and Red Allen," *Dayton Voice*, March 19, 1997.

12. Rob Modic, "2 Free of Rape Convictions, Released; 11 Years in Prison End on Teary Note; They Thank Supporters," *Dayton Daily News*, March 9, 1996.

13. Martin Yant, "Three of the Six Who Testified against a Couple for Sexual Abuse 10 years Ago Now Say: 'It Didn't Happen.' But Two People Remain in Prison. For Life," *Dayton Voice*, August 25, 1994.

14. Marianne McMullen, "After 11 Years, Jenny Wilcox's and Dale Aldridge's Cry for Justice Is Finally Heard in the Montgomery County Courthouse," *Dayton Voice*, February 21, 1996.

15. Richard Ofshe and E. Walters, *Making Monsters: False Memories, Psychotherapy, and Sexual Hysteria* (New York: Charles Scribner's Sons / MacMillan Publishing, 1994).

16. Lawrence R. Frey and Kevin M. Carragee, eds., *Communication Activism* (Cresskill, NJ: Hampton Press), vol. 1: 2007, vol. 2: 2007, vol. 3: 2012.

17. John P. McHale, "Unreasonable Doubt: Using Video Documentary to Promote Justice Communication Activism: Media and Performance Activism," in *Communication Activism*, vol. 2: *Media and Performance Activism*, edited by Lawrence R. Frey and Kevin M. Carragee (Cresskill, NJ: Hampton Press, 2007), 195–222.

18. Jack Newfield, *The Education of Jack Newfield* (New York: St. Martin's Press, 1980), 199.

19. Marianne McMullen, "Hohman Workers Walk out of High-Risk Workplace," *Dayton Voice*, December 4, 1996.

20. Marianne McMullen, "Hohman's Hazmat Blues," *Dayton Voice*, December 18, 1996.

21. Upton Sinclair, *The Jungle* (New York: Grosset and Dunlap, 1906).

22. Studs Terkel, *Working: People Talk about What They Do All Day and How They Feel about What They Do* (New York: New Press, 1972).

23. McMullen, "Hohman's Hazmat Blues."

24. Marianne McMullen, "The Power to Care," *Dayton Voice*, June 25, 1997.

25. McMullen, "The Power to Care."

26. Marianne McMullen, "Hohman Fined, Contract Signed," *Dayton Voice*, February 26, 1997.

27. Marianne McMullen, "Franciscan Votes Down Union, Nurses Vow to Try Again," *Dayton Voice*, July 2, 1997.

28. US Department of Agriculture, Federal Meat Inspection Act, Subchapters 1 through 5, Food Safety and Inspection Service, https://www.fsis.usda.gov/policy/food-safety-acts/federal-meat-inspection-act.

29. Mark Cook, "Homicide in Progress," *Dayton Voice*, April 2, 1997.

30. Tim Eubanks, "Racist Image," letter to the editor, *Dayton Voice*, April 9, 1997.

31. Debra Juniewicz, "Voice Cover Sparks Controversy over Racial Images," *Dayton Voice*, April 9, 1997.

32. Jeff Epton and Marrianne McMullen, "An Apology," *Dayton Voice*, April 9, 1997.

33. Jeff Epton and Marrianne McMullen, "Goodbye Dayton: Newspaper Co-publishers and Co-founders Move on to Chicago," *Dayton Voice*, December 23, 1999.

PART 3

1. Gordon Lafer and Lola Loustaunau, "Fear at Work: An Inside Account of How Employers Threaten, Intimidate, and Harass Workers to Stop Them from Exercising Their Right to Collective Bargaining," report by the Economic Policy Institute, July 23, 2020.

2. Hospital Report Card and Discriminatory Pricing Reform Act, Illinois General Assembly bill summary, January 1, 2004, https://www.ilga.gov/legisla tion/ilcs/ilcs3.asp?ActID=2466&ChapterID=21.

3. Michelle Rogers, "Under Siege: Hospitals Fend off Hardball Union Tactics," *HealthLeaders*, January 2004, 55.

4. *Chicago Sun Times*, "Less Helpful Hospitals," July 4, 2004, 11.

5. Chris Kutalik, "Two Unions Enter Recognition Pact with Health Care Company," *Labor Notes*, June 30, 2003.

6. Francine Knowles, "Nursing Home Union Hits Exec Pay," *Chicago Sun-Times*, March 29, 2005, 58.

7. Charlotte Ryann and Karen Jeffreys, "Challenging Domestic Violence: Trickle-Up Theorizing about Participation and Power in Communication Activism," *Communication Activism: Media and Performance Activism*, vol. 3, edited by Lawrence R. Frey and Kevin M. Carragee (Cresskill, NJ: Hampton Press, 2012), 185.

8. Laura Whittington, "Unions Split in Illinois Primary: Obama, Hynes Vying for Senate Backing," *Roll Call*, November 12, 2003.

9. Scott Fornek, "Obama Defeats Hull's Millions, Hynes' Name; Consistent Effort Results in Landslide for Hyde Parker," *Chicago Sun Times*, March 17, 2004, 10–12.

10. Fornek, "Obama Defeats Hull's."

11. National Aeronautics and Space Administration, "Total Lunar Eclipse," October 13, 2004, https://science.nasa.gov/science-news/science-at-nasa/2004 /13oct_lunareclipse.

12. Jason George, "Farm Aid Expenses Eat Away at Donations; Only 28% of Revenue from Last Year Made It to Farm Families," *Chicago Tribune*, September 17, 2005, 1.

13. Don Wycliff, "Watching How Money Flows: Farm Aid Officials Claim Tribune Article 'Mislead the Public about Farm Aid's Financial History,'" *Chicago Tribune*, September 29, 2005, A29.

14. Daniel Wagner, "Kim Gordon Talks about Her Favorite Song," *New York Times Magazine*, October 9, 2019.

15. Greg Hinz, "SEIU, Addus Health Care to Sign New Contract Friday," *Crain's Chicago Business*, January 26, 2006, https://www.chicagobusiness.com /article/20060126/NEWS/200019315/seiu-addus-health-care-to-sign-new-con tract-friday.

16. Robert Novak, "Hoffa and Stern Have Rejected Organized Labor's Political Illusion," *Chicago Sun-Times*, July 28, 2005, 41.

17. Barb Kucera, "Thousands Join 'Take Back Labor Day' at Harriet Island Festival," *Twin Cities Daily Planet*, September 2, 2008, https://www.tcdailyplan et.net/thousands-take-back-labor-day-harriet-island-festival/.

18. Service Employees International Union, "SEIU Members Launch Take Back Labor Day Caravan in St. Louis," SEIU press release, August 26, 2008, https://www.seiu.org/2008/08/seiu-members-launch-take-back-labor-day -caravan-in-st-louis.

19. Seth Woehrle, "Tom Morello, Mos Def Narrowly Avoid a Riot at Minnesota's Take Back Labor Day Concert," *Rolling Stone*, September 2, 2008, https:// www.rollingstone.com/politics/politics-news/tom-morello-mos-def-narrowly -avoid-a-riot-at-minnesotas-take-back-labor-day-concert-246772/.

20. International Institute for Sustainable Development, "Summary Report, 1-12, December 2008: Poznan Climate Change Conference," December 2008, https://enb.iisd.org/events/poznan-climate-change-conference-december -2008/summary-report-1-12-december-2008.

21. Kevin Doyle, "More from the National Green Jobs Conference," *Grist*, March 20, 2008.

PART 4

1. "Total Number of Charter Schools in the United States from 2000/01 to 2021/22," Statista Research, https://www.statista.com/statistics/236210/numb er-of-charter-schools-in-us/#:~:text=In%20the%202021%2F22%20school ,schools%20in%20the%20United%20States.

2. National Alliance for Public Charter Schools, table of total number of charter school students, and table of total number of charter schools, from 2005 to 2021, updated December 6, 2022, https://data.publiccharters.org /digest/charter-school-data-digest/how-many-charter-schools-and-students -are-there/.

3. S. Farkas, J. Johnson, and A. Duffett, "Stand by Me: What Teachers Really Think about Unions, Merit Pay and Other Professional Matters," report on a national survey (New York: Public Agenda), June 1, 2003, https://policy commons.net/artifacts/1175108/stand-by-me/1728237/.

4. Parent Revolution's website: https://www.parentrevolution.org.

5. Bruce Randolph School's website: https://brucerandolph.dpsk12.org.

6. Melanie Asmar, "Denver Weighs Tension between School Autonomy and Teacher Protections," *Chalkbeat*, September 28, 2020, https://co.chalk beat.org/2020/9/28/21492629/denver-innovation-schools-autonomy-vs -teacher-job-protections.

7. Asmar, "Denver Weighs Tension."

8. Fast Company Staff, "Update: Michelle Rhee vs. DC Teachers Union," *Fast Company*, February 1, 2010.

9. Mike DeBonis, "Michelle Rhee Explains Fast Company Quote," *Washington City Paper*, January 26, 2010.

10. *Washington Post* editorial, "Michelle Rhee Must Open Up about References to Unfit Teachers," *Washington Post*, January 26, 2010, A14.

11. Bill Turque, "Rhee Silent on Details of Abuse Claims against Ex-Teachers," *Washington Post*, January 26, 2010, B1.

12. Bill Turque and Jon Cohen, "Rhee's Approval Rating in Deep Slide," *Washington Post*, February 1, 2010, B1.

13. Digital Learning Collaborative, accessed October 4, 2023, https:// www.digitallearningcollab.com/dlc-awards.

14. "United They Fall: DC Mayor Adrian Fenty and His Schools Chief, Michelle Rhee, Are Linked in the Public Mind. These Days, That's Bad News for Both of Them," *Express*, a publication of the *Washington Post*, February 1, 2010, cover story.

PART 5

1. Jerry Markon, "Funds Denied to Bishops' Group the Latest Flare-Up," *Washington Post*, November 1, 2011.

2. Markon, "Funds Denied to Bishops' Group."

3. Stephanie Mencimir, "Catholic Church Loses Big Battle over Contraception," *Mother Jones*, March 26, 2012.

4. Manny Fernandez, "Base Serves as Home for Children Caught at Border," *New York Times*, April 28, 2012.

5. Abe Levy, "Local Groups Organize to Help Immigrant Children," *San Antonio Express-News*, August 7, 2014.

6. Restless Spirit blog post (anonymous), "Heads up Marrianne," January 23, 2014.

7. Restless Spirit blog post (anonymous), "Heads up Marrianne."

8. Christ Parsons, Melissa Harris, and Katherine Skiba, "Penny Pritzker Nominated for Commerce Secretary," *Chicago Tribune*, May 2, 2013, https:// www.chicagotribune.com/news/ct-xpm-2013-05-02-chi-penny-pritzker-co mmerce-secretary-20130502-story.html.

9. The Office of Child Support Enforcement name was changed to the Office of Child Support Services under the Biden administration in June 2023. See

Federal Register, vol. 88, no. 107, p. 36587, https://www.govinfo.gov/content/pkg/FR-2023-06-05/html/2023-11815.htm.

PART 6

1. Nelson Algren, *Chicago: City on the Make* (Oakland, CA: Angel Island Publications, 1961).

2. Alex Kotlowitz, *Never a City So Real: A Walk in Chicago* (Chicago: Chicago University Press, 2019).

3. Richard Rhodes, *Hell and Good Company: The Spanish Civil War and the World It Made* (New York: Simon and Schuster, 2015), xvii.

4. Cade Metz, "The 'Godfather of A.I.' Leaves Google and Warns of Danger Ahead: For Half a Century, Geoffrey Hinton Nurtured the Technology at the Heart of Chatbots like ChatGPT. Now He worries It Will Cause Serious Harm," *New York Times*, May 1, 2023.

5. Philip Marcelo, "Fact Focus: Fake Image of Pentagon Explosion Briefly Sends Jitters through Stock Market," Associated Press, May 23, 2023.

6. Emily Bender, Timnit Gebru, Angelia McMillan-Major, Schmargaret Schmitchell, "On the Dangers of Stochastic Parrots: Can Language Models Be Too Big?" *Association for Computing Machinery*, March 1, 2021.

7. Everett M. Rogers, *Diffusion of Innovations*, 5th ed. (New York: Simon and Schuster, 2003).

8. Ronald E. Rice and Charles K. Atkin, *Public Communication Campaigns*, 4th ed. (Newbury Park, CA: Sage Publications, 2013).

9. Jennifer Asenas, Bryan J. McCann, Kathleen Feyh, and Dana Cloud, "Saving Kenneth Foster: Speaking with Others in the Belly of the Beast of Capital Punishment," *Communication Activism: Media and Performance Activism*, vol. 3, ed. Lawrence R. Frey and Kevin M. Carragee (Cresskill, NJ: Hampton Press, 2023), 264.

10. Diffusion of Innovation Theory was developed by E.M. Rogers in 1962. More at https://sphweb.bumc.bu.edu/otlt/mph-modules/sb/behavioralchangetheories/behavioralchangetheories4.html.

11. Stuart L. Esrock, Joy L. Hart, and Greg Leichty, "Smoking out the Opposition: The Rhetoric of Reaction and the Kentucky Cigarette Excise Tax Campaign," in *Communication Activism: Media and Performance Activism*, vol. 1, ed. Lawrence R. Frey and Kevin M. Carragee (Cresskill, NJ: Hampton Press, 2007), 397.

12. Albert Salvato, "National Briefing, South: Kentucky: Push to Raise Cigarette Tax," *New York Times*, January 8, 2005.

13. Multiple studies have debunked the effectiveness of myths and facts messages. One of the best is a 2007 study by Norbert Schwarz and colleagues that tested a myths and facts patient handout developed by the Centers for Disease Control and Prevention (CDC) to counter common myths about the flu vaccine.

"Making the Truth Stick and the Myths Fade: Lessons from Cognitive Psychology," accessed November 17, 2023, https://behavioralpolicy.org/wp-content/uploads/2017/05/BSP_vol1is1_Schwarz.pdf.

14. Kellie Randall, Marrianne McMullen, and Matthew Morton, "Disseminating Research to Human Service Professions: Results of a National Survey" (Chicago: Chapin Hall, 2022), https://www.chapinhall.org/research/human-service-providers-communications.

15. *National Journal, Washington in the Information Age*, https://www.nationaljournal.com/bp/659170/washington-in-the-information-age.

16. Randall, McMullen, and Morton, "Disseminating Research."

Index

About the Author

Marrianne McMullen is a communications professional in public affairs who has worked in all sectors of the economy: private (journalist), public (DC Schools; Obama administration), nonprofit (labor unions), and academia, where she is currently director of communication at the Chapin Hall research center at the University of Chicago. She has a BS in journalism from West Virginia University and an MA in communications from the University of Dayton.